Woolley Colliery - Ar it woh

Memories of a village life lost

Edited by Judy Speight and Joyce Parling, with Jayne Dowle

Strongly supported by Dave Bogg, Billy Crossley, Jen James, Doreen Sykes and Olive Whittles.
Thanks to all our contributors and supporters who have been so generous with their time and money, and to Councillor Roy Miller. Special thanks to Luke Devine and Kate Wooffindin of Body Language (Barnsley Ltd), Posh Skincare Ltd and Posh Hair Ltd.

This book was funded by the Coalfields Regeneration Trust and Darton and Dodworth Area Forum.

Supported by

the **coalfields** regeneration trust

BARNSLEY
Metropolitan Borough Council

First edition.
First published in December 2007 by
Woolley Colliery Locality Study Group

ISBN 978-0-9557971-0-1

Designed by Mark Hutchinson and printed by
PHP Litho Printers, Barnsley, 01226 785811

Contents

Preface

In this introduction I want to provide a little of the background to which our memories of mining communities are connected. There have been hardship, poverty and tears but there are also the strong family ties, the unity and the solidarity.

Woolley Colliery, along with the other pits which existed close by, had an enormous economic and social and cultural impact on the locality. The colliery was sunk towards the end of the 19th century and remained in production for most of the 20th.

The mining industry generally had a plentiful supply of labour. Shortly before the start of the First World War it employed almost 1.2 million miners. Their working day was hard and dangerous. The coal was 'hand got' for the most part because there was little mechanisation. An abundance of labour kept wages low and it militated against innovation in the industry.

The area surrounding Woolley Colliery was dominated by the mining industry for more than a century and a half. Once, which-ever direction you looked in from Woolley Colliery village the spoil heaps rose like giant carbuncles on the landscape.

From being one of the biggest pits in Yorkshire, Woolley Colliery was dramatically run down until it finally closed in the early 1990s. When the miners' strike started in 1984, it employed more than 1,700 men. By December 1985 there was a workforce of 1,204. By December 1987 this was down to 659. This dwindled to just 68 men in December 1989.

During the strike community solidarity was strengthened both nationally and internationally. Women played an active role in defending miners' jobs. The Women Against Pit Closures movement was formed in Barnsley in the very early days of the strike. It mobilised women in a way not experienced before in an industrial dispute and it provided many with a totally new horizon.

Now, in 2007, the nearest colliery to Barnsley is 18 miles away and in the entire country there are only six working collieries. At the same time the country imports more than 35 million tonnes of coal per year for electricity generation.

Michael Clapham, M.P. for Barnsley West and Penistone

Introduction

There are lots of happy memories associated with living and growing up in Woolley Colliery village which describe how hard but uncomplicated post-war life was in this once thriving community. It was unique, a close-knit place where everyone knew everyone.

Two years ago, at the suggestion of Bob Hudson, a group of people born and raised in Woolley Colliery gathered together for a meeting with a view to record these precious memories.

Over the years the life and soul of the village has slowly been drained mainly with the closure of the pit, followed by the school, the demolition of the institute and church and finally the loss of the few amenities that were there, including the fish and chip shop and village shop.

Change was inevitable as people were forced to move to find employment - just as work had brought their grandparents to the pit in the first place.

New housing is now encroaching on the place where the pit winding gear once proudly stood. The village faces more changes and could lose its identity completely.

This book is a snapshot in time which remembers the people and their life in this special village and, we hope, will forever keep alive the memories of such a very special place and time in history.

Judy Speight, nee Tear and Joyce Parling, nee Brown

I loved the walks in the surrounding woods and up on to Woolley Edge and the freedom we all seemed to have at the time. The pit was the reason for the village's existence and it provided work for its inhabitants. It was a solid, gutsy lively community with a diversity of characters.
Carol Brown, nee Shaw

Woolley Colliery was a tiny mining community in a little fold below Woolley Edge. The only road in and out was over the lane from Darton. Colliery kids never really went very far, we played in and around the village. Up in the woods, in the fields, down at the bus station, or on the lane, up the Ladysmith and onto the Welfare. Sometimes we ventured up to Brick Row where a lot of us had been born, also, Horsfields' farm at Windhill was visited, we were sent for taties and tonjies (turnips).

We had the shop, the chip 'oil, the 'stute, the church and the school. Butchers' vans came round weekly, also Stephen Dunford the greengrocer, a hardware van called on a Friday afternoon and we got our rations from Darton Co-op on a Friday and mam went to Barnsley Market on a Saturday teatime for fruit and fish.

We were in our own little world. In the background the pit worked on; the buzzer hooted; the wagons shunted; the lorries were loaded, and the miners worked on.

Folk from t' Colliery just got on with it.

Marion Brackin, nee Coatesworth

Our schooil

A went to t'Colliery schooil tha knows
Thru wind an rain an severe snows,
Aye wi booits an clogs an wellies too,
But they wear trainers these days an' fancy shoes.
Above the village, at top o' t' hill,
Stands me owd schooil so proud and still,
If wi wo late an 'eard the bell,
We used to make us legs run like hell,
We nivver ivver liked being late.
As we used to try an be first at t'gate.
Na we hear ar schooil's to close,
Some negative thinking somewhere a suppose.
They can't take away ar childhood days,
Won't ever erase ar pit village ways.
In field beside woodland ar little schooil stood,
Among bluebells, wild roses, hearts of oak and beechwood.
Tha could hear skylarks an blackbirds on' t' way t'schooil,
Tha'll nivver forget, or tha must be a fooil.
From Moorhouse and Brick Row the kids used to come,
Remember far Moorhouse? it's now kingdom come!
The schooil and the pit where most of us were born,
Among muck stacks an' coil dust and ripe fields of corn.
Please Lord why close ar children's schooil?
For them and us it's ever so cruel.
How many ave looked at the cross on the roof,
For years it as been theer ar guardian aloof,
And when all as gone forever in time,
For teachers and pupils may we ave a shrine,
Put t'old rugged cross weer schooil used ta be,
On this beloved green hill for ar memory.

W.J. Crossley (pupil, September 1947 to August 1952)

Time to think...

I keep having a ride up to Woolley to look around and all I see is this once beautiful playground being devoured by that 'monster' which the spin doctors call progress.

But after all that, if I had to come back on this earth again I would wish for a time capsule to take me back to the day I was born, 20 July 1940 and drop me off at number 79 Woolley Colliery.

Terry Taylor

Low Row and Bluebell Road nestled in the woods around 1990
(Boggs)

Joe Tear, *standing*, with Barbara and
Joyce Tear and Lilian Rich at
Moorhouse Farm in the 1920s
(Tears)

Portrait of a lady - Jane Tear,
Judy Speight's grandmother
(Tears)

Rogues' gallery, 1950 - *top,* Jackie Joyner, Eugene Senior, Billy Crossley, Jean Sargison, Valerie Lockwood,
Jen White, Valerie Garforth
Bottom, Stuart Rhodes, Alec Richardson, Roland Wiles, David Sanger, Tony Darker, Roy Hunter, Jeff Sager
(Tears)

Harvest Festival inside the old
Tin Missionary Church
(Bellin)

After the shift
(United Villages)

Two Joe Burbridges - father and son - at the Bottom
Old Row around 1937
(Boggs)

Chapter One
School Days
No-one ever forgets a good teacher - or a great school

The first school was built on the hill on the edge of Bluebell Wood in 1856.

...near the church which was just inside the wood where a hay chamber was converted into a school. It was above a stable in which nine horses were kept.

Bob Hudson

Education was not compulsory yet miners' and farm workers' children were encouraged to attend even though they could ill-afford the penny a week they were charged.

From 1870 the Government introduced a system of education that enabled local authorities to set up schools paid for out of the rates or taxes. This meant that all children between the ages of five and 13 could go to school if they paid about 2d (2 pence) a week.

Many people could still not afford to send their children to school. The teaching in these schools was often poor and undertaken by monitors who were only about 12 years old. Classes were large and often had more than 60 pupils.

More is known of a new school which was proposed in 1875 and opened in 1877 with 110 children, a good measure of how many families were now living in the mining village.

...the horses were moved to stables lower down the hill near to the end of the two old rows of houses to make way for the new school.

Bob Hudson

It seems that the school building was funded by Mr Wentworth of Woolley Hall.

...New School established for the benefit of the younger children. The new building has been erected at the expense of Mr Wentworth.

School very thin this week. Many parents not able to pay the school pence.

August 1880	*Report of Inspection.*
	Few scholars today in the upper standards as the children go to work here very young.
1881	*The fever continues to spread at the colliery and many of the children are thus prevented from attending school.*
1883	*Twenty four children away from school this morning most of them getting blackberries in the woods, several have been away four or five times this week.*
1884	*Many of the children are away this week potato picking, cutting turnips.*
1886	*The stove has been bad all day causing the air in the room to be full of sulphur and making it difficult to breathe. The gas has also smelt badly. The teachers have complained of it and I myself suffered severe headache.*

1886 Report

A thorough overhauling of the defective gas-pipes or whatever else is amiss is needed so that the fetid air of the room will be made fit to breathe. The structural defects pointed out two years ago should long since have been remedied, if not remedied, grants will be reduced.

Meeting the running costs of the school was dependent on grants from outside sources. Some came from the church, hence 'Woolley Colliery Church of England School'. If standards were not satisfactory, grants were lowered or stopped altogether.

September 1888	*The grant for English is again barely earned as intelligence is not well developed.*
October 1888	*In view of the strike I appealed to the managers (that is the Rev. Holland as corresponding manager) as to the course I must pursue in the event of the children coming to school without their pence.*

The manager of the Colliery replied with, 'I have to say that there will be no reason whatever why they should come without their pence today, as their fathers have all received their wages for the last week. Should however any come in such wise either this or on subsequent weeks, Mr Orby should use his discretion as to how far in each case the plea is a valid one, but on no account should he refuse admission in the case of any child because of the want of their school pence.

In 1891 the Government introduced free education for all children up to the age of 11 but consistency in their education was still often interrupted with strikes over pay.

September 1891	*Have not taken any school fees for two weeks, the managers having decided to accept the fee grant. Have received notice today that the school is to be quite free to the children.*
September 1893	*The attendance has been very poor and has not been so good as usual all week, the reasons being that many of the children are kept at home to gather coal.*
April 1894	*Re-opened the school after the holidays - very thin attendance, the reason for this being that a number of children are away from home, their parents being unable to support them, the colliery having been closed for some weeks. Work is very slack in the neighbourhood and on account of this the children are leaving the district. This is causing the attendance to be poor.*
July 1895	*Closed school for one month, in obediency to an order from the local sanitary authority, on account of the prevalence of scarlet fever and measles among the children.*

Extracts from the school's log paint a fascinating but depressing picture. Serious illnesses, poverty and deprivation were underlined by obvious class distinction between rich and poor.

In 1899 the school-leaving age was raised to 12. But many children still failed to attend school regularly, and continued to work during the day to help support their families.

Children were warned to come to school clean because many were 'ragged, dirty and verminous', with larva of vermin and ringworm. Serious illnesses such as diphtheria, whooping cough, typhoid, chicken pox and influenza were given as reasons for absence.

Young at Heart… around 1956-57
(Boggs)

Hitting 60 this year, the class of 1953-54
(Coatesworths)

Oh Happy Days… around 1956-57
(Unknown)

Memories… around 1954-55
(Coatesworths)

It's A Wonderful Life… around 1953-54
(Coatesworths)

…when I arrived at school very wet and cold after my walk from Moorhouse Farm. Miss Shaw used to dry my coat around the fire in the classroom. There was a fireguard.

Flo White, nee Tear

Miss Shaw was to become a legend. She was born about 1891 up Greenside, Staincross (1891 census). By the 1901 census she had moved with her family to Nephi Cottages near Bloomhouse Lane, Darton and was one of six children. She attended Woolley Colliery School, and in 1904, became a pupil teacher.

School Report 1921

Miss E. Shaw's conduct is highly satisfactory. Her excellent management of the Infants Department is indeed worthy of record. The children are enthusiastic and responsive, their progress being very good.
Not bad for an untrained teacher who began her career as a 'monitor' or pupil teacher training on the job!

…I was brought to this village in March, 1925. My brothers and sisters and I had our names entered into the register and allocated to various classes.

Mine, naturally, was Miss Shaw's and what an impression she had on me which I oft times carry with me to this day.

All the first finds, the flowers, the fruits, the berries, the nature lessons around the tree in the wood I experienced that first spring and summer at Woolley Colliery Church of England School.

In October, we started to concentrate and rehearse for the Xmas play or concert and party. I was with about nine or 10 little girls who did all the actions to the various incidents in the song. We would finish off by putting our hands on our hips and singng;-

'How d'ya like to be a baby girl?'

I said a poem about 'Little Sucker Thumb'
Jim Pem (Pendlebury) said a poem called: -
My Brothers

Those twins, those twins, those dreadful twins,

Those twins who look so good,

You'd never guess the mischief,

They would do if they could.

Who put the flour in the sink, the sugar in the stew?

And put the bluebag in the rinse to paint their noses blue?

Mr Whittingstall had asked all our mothers to bake buns and make sandwiches so after the concert we had our school Christmas party.

When I moved onto the older classes, how things changed. I couldn't understand how some of the older boys got away with some of their devilment. When the trams were running on the tramlines, they used to jump on and ride to Beamshaw, wait for another returning and come back down to school again. They got six of the best for being disobedient but the next day, the headmaster's cane was missing and no-one knew where it was. It had gone where the others had gone, between the window and the fireplace down a knot hole in the floor.

Truth be known, if the floor was lifted, there would be quite a number of canes in there.

Molly Tovey, nee Crossley

Lack of any or suitable footwear caused sores on feet in cold and snowy weather suggesting poverty, low wages and prolonged disputes with the colliery owners.

Several reports complained of the dismal and depressing condition of the fabric of the school building, the dirty décor and the run-down facilities. Complaints of the inadequate furniture and the lack of separate classrooms along with long periods without water and toilet facilities indicate how little had been done in 50 years.

…I was Miss Shaw's pet and because I could read very well she asked me to teach Leslie Routhledge. I nipped him under the table to make him concentrate.

Flo White, nee Tear

…at Christmas, Mr Wentworth of Woolley Hall sent a flat-bed cart and horses to school. All the children sat on the back and were taken to the Hall. There we were given a present from him and another present from his wife. It was a wonderful experience.

Flo White, nee Tear

And the effects of war were still evident in several ways.

…I started school at the age of three because my dad was in the army and I had two younger siblings. They took in younger children in these circumstances.

Olive Whittles, nee Brown

…I remember going to the muck stack behind Molly Tovey's the night they bombed Sheffield. I saw the search-lights, the guns and the kids in their siren suits.

May Newton, nee Crossley

…there was an air raid shelter between the school and the church which we were taken into - to practise what was expected of us during an air raid.

Bob Hudson

…it was an Anderson air raid shelter with soil, vegetation and debris all over it. We had air raid practices and we all had to go in this dark, dimly lit, damp and fusty shelter. SPOOKY!!!! I believe we wore gas masks, the younger ones had Mickey Mouse masks. They were in cardboard boxes with a string shoulder strap.

Jim Hudson

…we were shown how to fit them properly and on occasions a van came. We had to sit in the van with the masks on. We were told gas was in the van and if we had not put our masks on correctly it would leak and our eyes would run.

Bob Hudson

…the tape criss-crossed on the large windows was memorable.

Jenny Hepworth, nee Hudson

A coaster to commemorate the centenary of the school
(Crossleys)

Wood-side view of Woolley Colliery school in the 1980s
(Coatesworths)

The whole school in 1976
(Boggs)

WOOLLLEY COLLIERY COUNTY PRIMARY SCHOOL

Registration details for the following people:

16th day of March 1925

Ernest Crossley
Olive Blanch Crossley
Kathleen Crossley
Mary Lilian Crossley

5th day of July 1926

William Crossley

16th day of June 1930

Frank Crossley

7th day of May 1934

May Crossley

A family affair - the Crossleys go to school
(Crossleys)

The **1944 Education Act** raised the school-leaving age to 15 and provided universal free schooling in grammar, secondary modern and technical schools. Entry was based on the 11-plus examination. And still, Woolley Colliery Church of England School, now called Woolley Colliery County Primary School, had no electric lights, depended on a fire in the classroom for heat, a screen to divide it into two rooms, chemical toilets outside but:-

…school was brilliant… relaxed or what? I think Wakefield Council thought we were in Barnsley and Barnsley thought we were in Wakefield. No one seemed to bother or come and check what we were up to.

I remember marathon football games at lunch-time. We'd go out for lunch and the teachers just seemed to forget about us sometimes. Whether they were gossiping or busy or whatever but the bell would go for the end of lunch at about half past three, with the score 76 to 45 and all of us 'tired'. It was a merciful release. We'd go in, get dusted off and trip off home.

Don Rhodes

Attempts to supplement an inadequate and limited war-time diet were made by: -

…third-pint bottles of milk, full cream, handed out at milk break when, in extreme cold weather, the top of the milk would freeze which we sucked like a sweet—cod liver oil being given before milk, the milk to hopefully take away the taste.

Jim Hudson

…waiting in line for my dose of cod liver oil and orange juice, everyone using the same spoon, every day that was.

George Crossley

…In the bad winter of 1947 we were walking to school in ankle socks with snow up to our knees. The children from Brick Row had to dry their socks on the fire guard around the roaring fire in Miss Lee's classroom. Hardly anyone had Wellingtons and trousers for girls were unheard of.

Joyce Parling, nee Brown

…I can remember my dad carrying me up the wood-side to school because it was deep enough to cover me.

Doreen Sykes, nee Wraithmell

…so cold in 1947 that the milk was put by the fire to thaw but it never did as open fires go dead when it snows.

Billy Crossley

…but in summer it often tasted sour and it took a lot of getting down but you had to drink it all, sitting at your desk. We had our own spoon for cod liver oil, each one had a different-coloured piece of cotton wrapped around the handle. Sometimes I had the job of washing the smelly spoons!

Joyce Parling, nee Brown

The fear of the nit nurse finding nits was real for both mothers and children. Finding nits or scabies was a slur on the cleanliness of the family and was taken very seriously. You could tell if she found a serious case of scabies because she ordered the head to be shaved, covered in gentian violet and the kid had to wear a bonnet in the classroom.

…the morning ritual of a nit inspection before setting off to school. The fine-toothed nit comb was no problem for me and my brother with our short back and sides but it was a nightmare for my sister with her plaits.

Bob Hudson

…lots of people developed itchy dry skin patches called scurf. If you had these you had to take a red capsule.

Joyce Parling, nee Brown

And attempts to improve privacy and lessen noise in between the classrooms were made:-

…a classroom divider, half glass and half wood between Miss Shaw's room and Mr Wittingstall's.

Jim Hudson

…at Christmas the partition was rolled back for the Christmas party. We all had to take our own food and a cup and plate. We loved the party. We played the Grand Old Duke of York among other games. I seem to remember one year Sir William and Lady Sutherland came and gave us all a ball and sixpence.

Olive Whittles, nee Brown

But nothing could be done to improve the outdoor toilet facilities:-

… Wooden seats and buckets! Every week Jack Bannister came to empty them out with his horse and cart.

George Crossley

…the boys had an urinal, roofless walls to pee against. The challenge was to pee over the wall and I'm proud to say I was the only one to manage it in my time! The girls got the luxury of sitting down in a row of six chemical toilets, each of which had a pipe extruding from the building to the rear. In summer, when the grass was long, some of the boys would get a long piece of sword grass and manipulate it up the pipe to shock the girls mid-stream.

Don Rhodes

All of which paints a grim and unsavoury picture of school life in the 1940s and 1950s. But the miserable conditions were far outweighed by the warmth, fun and relaxed atmosphere created by teachers' lessons but mostly by the children themselves. They had little, expected nothing and accepted all that was offered.

…a hand bell was rung each morning in the playground to signal the start of the school day. It could be heard all through the village.

Jim Hudson

Playing out with the school in the background, *from left*, Donald Ward, Doreen Wraithmell, Heather Senior and Eugene Senior
(Wraithmells)

Jim Brown - no gardener he - with the school in the background
(Browns)

Billy Crossley aged 10 in 1952
(Crossleys)

Front view of the school around 1993
(Unknown)

Woolley Colliery - *Ar it woh*

…it's Miss Coy I remember most, by her dress which was a brown skirt and a pink blouse. The skirt was always high above her waist. Her hair was parted down the middle with two plaits, like earphones at the side.

May Newton, nee Crossley

…Miss Lee followed Miss Coy. I loved the nature walks with her. She taught me most of all I know about wildflowers, grasses, brackens and trees. She was a strict disciplinarian.

Billy Crossley

…my time in Miss Lee's class was very short. I can only remember doing sewing and embroidery. I didn't like her because she had favourites and made it obvious.

Olive Whittles, nee Brown

…I was eight and Miss Lee allowed two of us to make a nightdress in pale green wincyette. She let the other girl embroider her initial on the yoke, but I wasn't allowed to. Mine had to stay plain. There were many more instances of her meanness too painful to remember.

Joyce Parling, nee Brown

…I don't think Miss Lee liked me because all I seemed to do was write lines. I always got caught out when I did anything wrong. It was alright staying in the classroom in winter because there was a lovely fire but in summer I wanted to play out with everybody else.

Doreen Sykes, nee Wraithmell

…the country dancing classes run by Miss Lee were an ordeal, for the boys especially. As we changed partners, some girls were held closer than others.

Don Rhodes

…we had our games lessons in the field below the school. I can remember bean bags, hoops and coloured braids. That field is part of the wood now.

Joyce Parling, nee Brown

It is difficult to convey the depth of respect Miss Shaw commanded - and for so many years!

…my teacher was Miss Shaw, a tiny, kind lady with grey hair and glasses.

Joyce Parling, nee Brown

…her classroom always seemed cosy as there was a real fireplace in the corner. It was there I learned to knit on large wooden needles and scraps of wool.

Jenny Hepworth, nee Hudson

This warmth is echoed throughout everyone's recollections. Miss Shaw would surely have been elevated to the 'Teacher of the Decades' if such an accolade had existed in those days.

Considering she was untrained, she had a huge influence on many young people's lives.

She began her career in 1905 and retired in 1952. All those generations…!

…at playtime we had normal boundaries, one of them being Miss Shaw's tree. It had bark missing at the base in the shape of a small door - for what? Elves? It added to the mystery but just imagine having a tree named after you! What an honour!

Don Rhodes

…on my first day in Miss Shaw's class my mum took me and left me in the playground but she would find me on the doorstep waiting for her by the time she got home. This happened a few times so I had to go to Miss Shaw's house and go to school with her.

Doreen Sykes, nee Wraithmell

…in the summer, Miss Shaw would take all her class and sit around a chestnut tree in the wood for lessons. The tree is still there today and is called Miss Shaw's tree.

Dave Bogg

…my favourite time was the afternoons when Miss Shaw would take out the large blue-coloured hard-backed book and read to us 'Peter Pan' - still my favourite story.

Jean Jones, nee Rhodes

…nature walks to Miss Shaw's tree and the first finds of wild plants and flowers of the year, (bird's foot trefoil was the commonest find) - we got praise.

Olive Whittles, nee Brown

…loved Christmas, with Miss Shaw showing us how to make Chinese lanterns from wallpaper, and raffia work with the old-fashioned cardboard bottle tops with the centre pushed out of them.

Billy Crossley

…hung across the classroom to dry. As we got older we made lovely Christmas balls out of what seemed like hundreds of round coloured-paper pieces folded like a paper dart then threaded together by needle and cotton creating a ball.

Joyce Parling, nee Brown

…and we made a cracker and Miss Shaw put a threepenny bit in the cracker. These always went on the Christmas tree at home.

Olive Whittles, nee Brown

…at Easter, if we had a spare egg, we took it to school and Miss Shaw taught us how to paint and decorate them. She read us stories about Jesus from a Bible.

Bob Hudson

…tried to teach us manners and etiquette. I particularly remember handkerchief drill when everyone had to hold out their right hand at arms' length with a hanky or piece of cloth held between thumb and forefinger, reciting, 'Coughs and sneezes spread diseases, so use your handkerchief please'.

Jean Jones, nee Rhodes

Janet Farnsworth washing her smalls
(Farnsworths)

Protests against the closing of our school in 1993 - sad memories
(Margisons)

A sweet chestnut for a sweet Miss Shaw
(Boggs)

"Not one of us had ever seen Miss Shaw but we all knew of her and followed her lead. Visitors were always escorted to her tree and her story told," Jack Mills

WOOLLEY COLLIERY SCHOOL FORMER PUPILS ASSOCIATION

Dear Friend,

It is with regret we have to inform you that, because of the resignation of the Secretary and Treasurer - due to personal commitments - it has been decided to suspend activities of the above Association.

A special meeting was advertised in the Barnsley Chronicle for 15th September but was poorly attended, hence this letter. If you are interested in taking office as Hon. Secretary or Hon. Treasurer, please contact any person named below.

In closing, we the members of the previous Committee would like to thank you for your support at our re-union Dinners, etc. and hope this support will not be lost forever.

Yours sincerely,

THE COMMITTEE.

Mr. L. Sagar, 32 Hawthorne Street, Shafton, Barnsley. 710665
Mr. E. Tear, The Flat, Station Road, Darton 2147
Mr. & Mrs. H. Turner, 114 Woolley Colliery, Darton 4409
Mr. G. Child, 11 Windhill Ave, Darton 5440
Mr. & Mrs. D. Tovey, 27 Bluebell Road, Darton
Mr. W. Sellars, 40 Cooper Road, Kexbro - Darton 5823
Mr. G.H. Watson, 9 Station Road, Darton 2975

The end of an era - letter from the mid-1960s
(Toveys)

"May God bless, guard, guide and sustain these children and all those whose hearts and minds contain memories of this enchanted place," - quote from the last headmaster, Mr Jack Mills
(Margisons)

...she kept sand in sand-bags and at certain times she would spread the sand out on a cover and allow us to play in the sand on a rota basis.

Dave Bogg

...with large sea shells for you to hear the sea and boxes full of smaller ones to help us learn to count.

Jim Hudson

...but if you were naughty her hand hurt when she spanked your bare legs.

Billy Crossley

...I remember Miss Shaw's retirement in 1952. She was presented with an easy chair. She was broken-hearted.

Billy Crossley

...yet even in her later years, after retirement, Miss Shaw, that very kind, tiny, grey-haired lady with an owl face (due to her round black spectacles) maintained an interest in the school and all its pupils. I can still hear her quiet but sharp, eloquent but raspy voice sounding like comfortable slippers being dragged over gravel.

Phillip Crossley

Other fond and special recollections were sparked by visual aids pinned around the classroom walls or by precious moments which seemed insignificant at the time.

...learning the alphabet from a board divided into four squares, starting A,B,C,D, then moving on in fours until the end of the alphabet.

Joyce Parling, nee Brown

...boxes of coloured spots drawn permanently on Miss Shaw's blackboard. They were arranged one spot to 12. We learned our times tables parrot fashion from the boxes. They have helped me enormously throughout my life. I've never forgotten them.

Olive Whittles, nee Brown

...we played with Plasticine, coloured chalks and wooden jigsaw puzzles in MrWinstanley's class. We collected labels off tins of food from other countries. We matched them up to countries shown on a large map on the wall.

Bob Hudson

...when Mr Geldard was headmaster he walked to school from Woolley Village and we walked up the wood-side to meet him. He gave us mental arithmetic tests every Friday morning and Malcolm Rhodes was always first to answer.

Joyce Parling, nee Brown

...after walking two miles from Moorhouse Farm on Monday morning, I was sent back immediately to get the teachers' eggs. Why didn't they tell me on Friday how many to bring?

Jen James, nee White

...Sports Day was in the field below the school. It was like a switchback. We were running up hill and down dale, but like everything else, it was great fun.

Olive Whittles, nee Brown

...in 1949 I was a member of the church choir along with Mick Brown, Granville Booth, Bachus Wraithmell and Hubert Joyner. The choirmaster was Arnette Empsall who took all the choir on a day trip to Scarborough for the day, on public transport. We took the bus to Barnsley, then on to Wakefield then to Leeds then York, finally on to Scarborough. Arnette had arranged for us to have a fish and chip lunch in a hotel that one of his relatives owned.

Dave Bogg

... Mr Walton became headmaster when I was in Standard 4. He was much younger than any headmasters we'd had before and like a new broom, he really did change things. He thought nothing of giving us a clip behind the ear or the cane (we probably deserved it!). He introduced the boys to gardening. They dug out big plots at the side of the school where they grew flowers and vegetables. The girls kept chickens and went around the village collecting scraps to feed them.

Joyce Parling, nee Brown

...we had an incubator with 36 eggs hatching in it. During the school holidays, Jack Joyner, Stuart Rhodes and me were given the school key and entrusted to turn the eggs twice every day.

Jen James, nee White

...Mr Walton introduced radio in our lessons and loved the fact that I was interested in 'The Planets Suite' by Gustav Holst. He also introduced inter-school sports to us which were held at Calder Grove, Wakefield.

Billy Crossley

Another memory which evoked strong feelings was the 11-plus.

...tension built as the 11-plus examination approached. I don't know if Mr Greenwood knew what the date was, but we certainly didn't - we just knew it was coming soon.

On the fateful day we were sitting petrified waiting for the papers to be doled out in our rows. There was a tense, deathly hush. One boy obviously had the wind up more than the rest of us because he let out the most enormous trump that reverberated round the classroom and set off gales of tension-relieving laughter. Thanks S.R..

Don Rhodes

We all used to go swimming to Scissett baths in the 1970s, where I passed my bronze, silver and gold badges. On the way we used to stop and pick up children from West Bretton school to fill up the bus. This was because both schools were very small so we had to share.

Neil Featherstone

Like the bows! - Geoff Ward and Joyce Brown
(Wards)

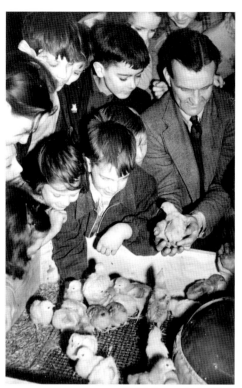

Mr Walton and his chicks
(Wards)

Just incubating - Mr Walton with Tony Mathieson, Mavis Ward, Marion Coatesworth and Wendy Mathieson
(Wards)

Neil Featherstone, *top row, far right*, with the school football team in the 1970s
(Featherstones)

We won the cup! The Woolley Colliery school sports team
(Featherstones)

Woolley Colliery - *Ar it woh*

Chapter Two
Laikin' art
A game for every season and a mate for every mood

What and where we played was very much governed by the time of year. Each season brought a change in temperature and length of day. This determined what pastime would be popular and whether we played indoors or out.

Marjory Whitehead, nee Child, says she'd love to laik art...

We played a lot in the woods, nesting, picking flowers and playing on the aerial flight in the wood near the school. We loved playing it so much that our turn didn't come soon enough. In Brick Row wood, there was a swing going over a deep ditch from one bank to another.

At weekends, in the summer and if the weather was good, **we used to walk past Beamshaw Pit and over the fields to Woolley Dam.** It was a very popular place. I swam across it once with my older brother. If we had any money we would go on a boat.

My best memories are of the winter when we had snow, going in the Welfare fields jumping in the snow drifts. **I had a pair of my brother's old trousers on and wellies.** Sometimes the snow was deeper than us, but we would struggle out and do it all again.

The sledging was marvellous. I had my brother's sledge he had made himself. The run started outside the school, went down the hill, past the houses, across the bus station and over the two wagon lines. **I went on my stomach and steered with my feet.** Then I trekked all the way back up and did it all again. It was great doing it in the moonlight, with the ice shining. We were not very popular with the adults because we made the road too slippery. If they wanted to go to the shop, they put a pair of socks on over their shoes.

My friend Shelia Loft lived in the big house. Her father was the manager at the pit. One Saturday afternoon, when we were about 10, her dad gave us a treat. He took us down the pit to see the pit ponies. **It was a bit scary going in the cage,** but we enjoyed the ride on the paddy train to the stables and we gave the ponies some sugar. My mother couldn't believe it.

The only thing I didn't like was that my dad kept pigs. When I came home from school I had to go with my bucket to certain houses who kept their peelings for us. I hated that because some kids made fun of me. **I was happy though when we killed a pig** and I used to take them some pork as a thank you.

Olive Whittles, nee Brown, can laik art her mam says...

My first memories are of slap dab, mixing muck with water, in old tin cans or jars and making 'cakes'. **We used the same jars for catching bees,** filling the jars with 'bee flowers' such as rosebay willow herb to attract them. As we waited, we dug a hole then tipped the flowers and the bees in. Finally, we covered them with glass. Poor bees... they always died!

Playing at weddings was always popular. **The giant empty corned beef cans snaffled from the bins near the pit canteen made ideal taxi seats** for the bride and bridesmaids. I still have the scar on my knee from one of those lethal cans. We loved the dressing-up part.

Playing schools was another group get-together but **Elizabeth Addy always had to be the teacher.** She would smack us hard and if we cried, she wouldn't let us go home. I can't think why we enjoyed playing schools so much.

We held concerts in the air raid shelter just above the Top Row. There was a large concrete top over a disused shaft on the small muck stack just above the school near the tramlines, **ideal for concerts and dancing.**

The Row end or bus station was where we all gathered to play Pig Jack Fly, nipsy, kick-out can or tigs. We used the gardens of the Bottom Row to play hide and seek, very exciting but a bit frightening after dark.

The black hut at the end of the Bottom Row gardens was full of big rolls of rubber belting of all sizes and we jumped from one to the other. It must have been quite dangerous.

There were bricks for pit use tipped in piles. We built buses, ships and cars, but houses were our favourite. **We had settees, tables, chairs and sideboards with a can of weeds.** We made cookers and even lit fires in them. We pretended to cook. Green elderberries were peas, pebbles were potatoes and slivers of rust from the girders were slices of meat. And of course, we had slap-dab cakes for afters!

The Dyke!!!! (River Dearne) - what wonderful summer days we spent there in the school holidays and weekends. **Anything passed for a 'cossy'.** Most of us learnt to swim there. 'Collery' kids swam at the Willow bend or the last bend near to Haigh. Darton kids swam at the Spring nearer to Darton. **We had to dam the water to get it deep enough** so not enough water flowed to the Spring for the Dartoners. Battles sometimes ensued!

We loved Bonfire Night. Logging occupied us for weeks before. Anticipation mounted as the date grew nearer. **We guarded the stacked bonfires to stop rivals pinching our logs.** The fire was all important because there were only a few fireworks.

We had snow that children today can only dream of. The excitement when it started was wonderful because we knew we would soon be able to start sledging. The runners on our home-made sledges had to be sandpapered to get rid of the rust and then we were away!

We lived in a mucky pit village but **it was a Mecca of play materials,** all supplied by the pit. I don't think any child had a more enjoyable childhood than the kids from 'Collery'. We didn't realise then just how lucky we were. Both woods were havens, bursting with bluebells in the spring which **we picked by the armful to take home to our mums.**

And her sister Joyce Parling, nee Brown, says she's coming an' all...

It was summer so the wood was a favourite place for playing at house. **We would sweep up leaf mould to make rooms,** play hide and seek, swing on trees, ride the aerial flight and, as we got older, flirt with the boys.

When Greeny, the local farmer, cut his hay field we had great fun piling it up and jumping on it, that is until he came with his shotgun!!! The top pond above school and the other one in Pie Wood near the Welfare **acted like magnets to beautifully-coloured dragonflies and us.** We fished for newts and collected frog spawn which we kept in a jar at home and waited for the tadpoles to emerge. Our Mick put some bleach in mine and killed them all.

The pit yard provided tubs to ride on, timber for making dens and for rafts on the raft pond. So many kids fell in and trudged home covered in slurry. We roller-skated at the bus station and tightrope-walked on thick rope wire by the wagons. As we got older, it became a meeting place for lads and lasses.

In the heat of summer, the pitch on the pavement would bubble up and we burst the bubbles, getting ourselves covered in tar. The only way to get it off was to rub on lard - **we must have smelled like bacon!**

If the lads were lucky enough to find four wheels off an old pram they made trolleys and let us ride on them. There were metal bars in the Piecing, used by the firemen for their hoses. **We used them like a trapeze:** held on tightly, somersaulted backwards, came upright,

The kids are alright! - *from left*, baby June Blackburn with Emma Carchill, Joyce Brown, Mick Brown, Olive Brown and Lesley Hunters
(Browns)

Local kids laikin' art at Horsfield's farm
(Tears)

Do you wanna be in ar gang?
David Taylor, Mick Sanger, *sitting middle*,
Lew Coatesworth, Mick Brown, Derek Sanger,
boy on shoulders, and Tiffy Butler, *on bank*
(Browns)

Toys'R'us Woolley Colliery style - the pit yard, supplier of play equipment to the kids of the village
(Unknown)

Pit bottom and still smiling - after their long shifts, miners enjoyed many pastimes including nipsy, fives and nurr and spell
(United Villages)

Jack Howard watches Nathan Jordan play nurr and spell in the 1920s
(Boggs)

Woolley Colliery - *Ar it woh*

somersaulted forwards and ended up with blisters on our hands. **We peggied up** (did handstands) and went over into the crab, performed cartwheels, often spending more time upside down than right way up!

In autumn we walked up the old lane to Brookie's farm and pinched pears. We went blackberry-picking in the hedgerows for jam and pies, sometimes with our mam.

As we got older we went peapicking and then potato-picking. **We got half a crown a day and a bucket of potatoes each day for our mam.** It was cold, wet, back-breaking work.

At the first sign of winter, the shop began a firework club and serious logging began. Not only did we have to find the wood, we had to drag it home and guard it. Every row had their own bonfire and wanted theirs to be the biggest and best so raiding parties were formed. Guarding was very important but scary as there were few street lights and **standing in the dark by yourself while others were raiding was no fun.**

Our weekly coppers at the shop mounted up. We aimed for half a crown so we could afford a box of mixed fireworks. **The lads preferred to buy bangers and jumping crackers** so they could chase us with them. On Bonfire Night we had jacket potatoes, pig hock, mushy peas, parkin and treacle toffee, all home-made. We kept the fire going for days and sat round it after school on our way home.

When I was eight, I got my first pair of wellies and couldn't wait for it to rain. I wore them so much that **I had a sore ring around each leg.** In winter, there was sledging from the school down to the bus station, ice skating on the ponds when the ice was thick enough and snowball fights. One year, when the snow froze, we were able to cut shapes out of the snow such as hearts and stars.

You didn't start playing out proper until you started school and making friends. Then we had 10 years of sheer bliss in the best playground ever dreamt of!

Dave Bogg sez he loves laikin' art...

In April we would all go bird-nesting into Woolley woods and to Moorhouse. We went a hell of a long way just to find nests. Frank Richmond was a farmer at the Haigh end of Moorhouse. **He didn't like kids.** Pebble Island on the River Dearne was on land he farmed and he was for ever giving us a bad time.

We visited the newt pond to catch newts or dragonflies. It was rare for us to go home dry and not sludged-up to the eyes. I can still hear my mother giving me earache.

In the winter we went to a variety of cinemas, mainly Darton Picture House or Mapplewell. If it was to be Barnsley then it would be the Ritz on Peel Street for the morning matinee or the Princess on Racecommon Road for the afternoon matinee. **The Ritz had a guy playing the organ before the films were shown.** The kids' show was called the ABC Minors.

If it snowed it was time to get out the sledges. We would start out by the school and come flying past the 'stute, down the concrete road, passing the Row end, over the landsale and weighbridge half way up the Ladysmith. **There was very little traffic.** The only thing we had to watch out for was the service bus. It was pretty hair-raising to see just how fast some of these sledges would go. **In really cold snaps, the ponds would freeze over** and we donned our skates (a pair of clogs) ready for action.

Snow and sledges weren't necessities to the resourceful kids from Colliery. At the back of the school and at the side of the 'Trammies' was a muck-stack - it's still there. **We found a bit of shelter tin,** bent it up at the front and used it to slide down the muck-stack. If the tin should stop suddenly it didn't do your backside or trousers any good.

If we wanted a bike we would go to the local tip in front of what was Edward's Glassworks (later BXL). It was always an advantage to have a pair of Wellingtons. Most of the bikes we built were fixed gear and without brakes, so **we needed to put a foot on the front tyre to stop them.**

Our parents took a dim view of this practice as our shoes very quickly wore out. Trollies were made of old pram wheels, always in short supply. We could get those trolleys to really trap, but they did not like being turned. If you tried this at speed, they would turn you completely over. **Gravel rash was an occupational hazard.** To fit steering you used a red hot poker heated in an open fire to burn holes for threading rope and fixing swivel bolts.

At the back of the present Low Row was an area the Coal Board used as a brick store. The bricks were just dumped out by a tipper lorry. Every kid must have played on these and got their fingers trapped. **It never stopped us going back even though the blood blisters did hurt.**

I always remember a Mr Hartshorne from my time living on the Old Row. He must have worked in one of the engineering workshops as he always seemed to have quite a stock of ball bearings which he used to pass around to us.

We played marbles at the row end (the bus station end of the Old Row) and sticks which included three sticks and a ball. **Pig Jack Fly was another game and** kick 'art (kick-out) can.

Woolley Colliery could have been the inspiration for Alton Towers. The rides and adventures certainly compared in both imagination and thrills. The pit provided all the materials we needed. Belting, bull-ropes, tub hooks, cabling and haulage ropes were dragged from the pit yard into the woods. A bull rope was tied to a tree (it's still there and in use) and **the best swing in the world was born** and christened 'the Big Dipper'.

In the timber yard there were tub lines going in all directions. We found a tub, pushed it like hell and then jumped into it. This happened once too often for Tony Whittaker, as his tub came off the track and **tipped completely over him.** It took me, Mick Sanger and Mick Brown to rescue him.

Some 'rides' took no work or imagination. In the timber yard at the back of the hay store was a pylon which supported an aerial flight and had guide cables anchored to the ground. These cables were about one inch thick and for some inexplicable reason, a pulley was left attached to one of these cables. The pulley was about 14 inches in diameter and was trapped on the cable so that it could not be removed. **It wasn't long before we found a use for it.** This cable came to the ground at an angle of about 45 degrees - quite steep. We attached a long rope then had about four of us pulling with one kid hanging underneath it. When it was at a reasonable height, we would let go and he would come hurtling to the ground. We took turns for two months and then **one day it was gone!** We never knew why.

We would get a heavy old haulage rope out of the pit yard and string it up between two trees using a Sylvester to tension it. Then we hooked a tub hook over the cable and used it to slide down. **There were two aerial flights,** both on the right of the path as you walk up towards Windhill.

The original aerial flight attracted kids from as far away as Mapplewell and Kexborough. We were going to Darton school so word quickly spread. The valley wasn't a natural valley but created from the old workings of the Bluebell pit which had collapsed.

The cable can be clearly seen, removed from its original position to where it is today. **It is extremely mind-blowing to see the remnants of this haulage rope** that we dragged into the wood from the timber yard so long ago.

We even had our own boating pool and water sport park: Woolley Dam. Several families would make the trip at the same time with a picnic lunch. It was a long walk and especially tough on the young kids but everyone returned home tired but very happy.

The River Dearne played a large part in our lives. On sunny days we would start out early morning and walk on the top Old Row calling at Goodalls' shop for a bottle of pop. **On cooler days we fished for minnows and crayfish,** with a fire lit to cook the crayfish.

Punch Douglas was in charge of the slurry ponds. He was, as his name implies, an ex-boxer. The Fountain and Burnley Coal Company had no use for fine coal dust, so had it pumped onto the stack near the Welfare. **It was like quicksand** and very difficult to get out of. This never stopped us and we had to be dragged out quite often.

"It wer a good day that," - 14-year old Dave Bogg playing on the beach at Withernsea in 1953
(Boggs)

Don't sit under the apple tree with anyone else but me - Jen White and David Tear
(Tears)

Girls just wanna have fun - Katrina, Jane and Yvonne Bogg playing out in 1969
(Boggs)

Best mates up to no good - at 16 Bluebell Road are Alan Bogg, Lew Coatesworth, Mick Sanger and Trevor Garforth
(Boggs)

Jen White with a lucky black cat
(Tears)

David Tear and Jen White - who scrumped all the apples?
(Tears)

The remains of the second aerial flight
(Boggs)

Messing about on the river - Jen White and Judy Tear
(Tears)

The raft pond was created by rain water siphoned off from as far as Woolley Edge, down the valley and trapped by the stack. It was never part of a reservoir or water from the slurry ponds. These were at the Welfare end of the stack.

To begin with **we built a raft mainly out of split bars** out of the pit timber yard and used a couple of 45 gallon empty oil drums to keep it afloat. Water would be absorbed into the split bars so that they became heavier than the water and would sink. It took a lot of time and effort to keep them afloat.

Then a stroke of luck! Woolley Dam had recently been drained. **All the rowing boats were surplus to requirements,** so they were brought into the pit timber yard. Holes were punched into their bottoms to render them useless but it didn't take us long to find them and do emergency repairs. We had a great time sailing on the raft ponds!

In August, for the Barnsley Feast two weeks' holiday, the pits had their annual shutdown. **The pit ponies would be brought out of the pit.** This was the highlight of the year as we got to ride them to their resting field as the horse handlers could not cope with so many horses - there could be as many as 80. They would be either taken on to the Ladysmith where the football field is, or to Pumma at the side of Darton Lane, just past Darton Primary School. **Pumma was a better bet as then the ride was longer.**

Day trips to the seaside were our holidays. All the fathers made sure that they were members of all the Working Mens' Clubs so that the kids got to go to the seaside as much as possible. In those days not many families, especially those who had lots of kids, could afford a week's holiday. We all looked forward to those day trips. **One trip to Cleethorpes from the Tin Hat in Mapplewell in the early 1950s took 89 buses.**

In the 1940s, at 6.45pm every weekday, the streets would be cleared of kids until 7pm. It was time for *Dick Barton Special Agent* with his trusty helpers Snowy and Jock. It didn't matter whose house you went into, just the nearest.

Families relied heavily on the radio programmes. We listened to Charles Chiltern's *Riders of the Range*, *ITMA* and *Much Binding In the Marsh* with Richard Murdock and Kenneth Horne. Sunday afternoon it would be the Forces' request programme and then Billy Cotton's *Band Show* and *Educating Archie* with Peter Brough.

Sunday morning would see us playing football in the field at the back of the Bottom Row. We would get ourselves kicked up in the air a few times and come off at the end of the match (which could have as many as 30 kids) with limps and bruises.

Rationing made life pretty grim. **Our parents saved ration coupons for extra sweets** at Christmas, but we had to go short the rest of the year. There were off-ration sweets though. You could get four CROMAX, a very strong lemon tablet, for a penny. We could also get a stick of 'Spanish' for 1/2d. We also had a sherbet dip called LINGO FIZZ which when sucked made your eyes go round (I'm sure they put soap powder in it).

My mother would never let us buy chewing gum because it needed too many coupons. There were all sorts of **chewing gums off ration but most tasted like candle wax.** One other thing that we used to relish was a stick of rhubarb dipped in sugar. It makes me cringe to even think about it now as I can't stand anything sour.

Marion Brackin, nee Coatesworth, wants to come an' all...

We had lovely picnics of jam or treacle sandwiches and a bottle of water. Crumbs always finished up in the water bottle but what the heck, we still drank it.

In winter we had a big sledge that held three people and a single one that was very fast. The first track was from school down to the tramlines, the second one from the top of Bluebell Road to the tramlines.

When the ponds froze over we skated. **One year the ice was thin and a boy fell in** and my cousin Mary had the presence of mind to take off her coat and threw it for him to grab hold of. I think she saved his life.

We played cricket up the field, dozens of us, with only loose rules. Girls could play to even up the side. **I never ever got to bat, was hopeless at catching,** but the lads tolerated us. Nipsy was a Sunday morning activity. There were all sorts of leagues: Barugh Green were the side to fear.

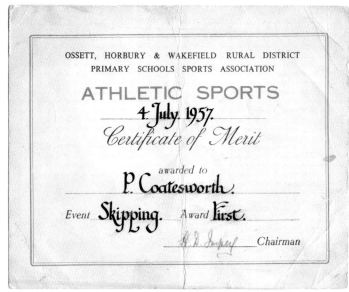

What a honour - Marion's sister Pat Coatesworth won because she "had the longest legs"
(Coatesworths)

Whips and tops had their seasons, but I preferred hoppy, either sixes or the aeroplane shape. **I was tall so could hop better than all my shorter mates.** Hop-scotches came in all guises. I used an old bacca tin full of pebbles, or pieces of shiny tile (dug out of old banking), any old flat stone would do so long as it slid into the right square.

It was mainly lads who were good at 'mabs', but our Betty was brilliant, our Mave wasn't so bad, but our **Betty Bly could win mabs off all the lads.** She had a drawstring Scotch-plaid bag, full to the brim with them. At bedtime, she would tip them all out onto the counterpane and say which ones she had won and off whom.

In the long holidays **we would take babies walks in their prams,** on to the Welfare and back. I once wheeled Josephine Waller, but she was mournjey, so home she went. I walked Michael White into the wood to pick celandines and wood anemones. He was a lovely little boy, **always nicely dressed in hand-knitted jerseys.** We went for long walks to Haigh, whole gangs of us, Sangers, Garforths. Jeannie (Garforth) often had to have their Frankie in tow, so was **dragged, cajoled, slapped, shouted at and eventually carried between us** most of the way, down the wood end path that skirted the wood to Primrose Hill, the pit and the muck stack to our left, through the field path to Moorhouse, past Richmond's farm and onto Haigh.

Sometimes we called at Aunt Liza's and Uncle Eric's for a drink of water. Aunt Liza never seemed fazed at **the sight of a dozen raggy kids on her doorstep,** and we often got treats, either spice or a bit of fruit. Course, it was kudos for me having rich relatives to call on. But I got played hell with if mam ever found out.

In August dozens of Colliery kids headed down through the pit yard, under the buckets that carried endless loads of muck to the slag heap. We always ran under them as someone once said they dripped 'hot stuff', so we didn't take any chances. **Down under the railway bridge, skirting the ripe wheat** and on to Pebble Island. The bigger ones who could swim well carried on to the last bend, where it was so deep they dove in head first. Roy Margison once had a leech fastened to his back, we were all terrified till a bigger lad knocked it off.

It's a fair cop - Barry Cooper and John Pendlebury
(Pendleburys)

Our family day out at Woolley Dam - Joe Tear with children Ernest, Joyce and Florence in 1927
(Tears)

Saddle up - Ian and Malcolm King
(Kings)

Summer fun - John Pendlebury on Low Row
(Pendleburys)

Woolley Colliery - *Ar it woh*

Skipping was good, sometimes the big lasses who were working would wind the rope for us during the long summer evenings. **It was a big thick rope, taken from the pit yard.**

"'All in together this fine weather'" was one of our favourites.

Pitch-patch-pine-pepper,

I know a nigger boy and he's double-jointed,

He gave me a kiss and made me disappointed,

He gave me another to match the other,

By gum Sheila, I'll tell your mother for kissing David Toll (or any boy's name) down by the river with a pitch-patch-pine-pepper.

Then you fast peppered for as long as possible.

All in together this fine weather - When I count two you've got to touch your shoe.

Then they would count one - two and you had to touch your shoe. When I count three you've got to touch your knee, one - two - three, then you had to touch your knee whilst carrying on skipping.

When I count six you've got to do the splits.

Two-four-six, then you all had to catch and stop the rope, those who failed were out.

If you go up the field to the first gate, the pond is in the field corner. Just beyond the pond the tram-lines take you up to Horsfield's farm. Many happy hours were spent here with our jam jars. There were newts and salamanders, like little dragons with their orange dappled skin. **The frog spawn became tadpoles and then young frogs, and we seemed to lose interest.**

Jen James, nee White, and Judy Speight, nee Tear, says they'll laik art an all...

We were lucky to have a magnificent sledge made at the pit to match the fantastic sledge run. Our sledge was so huge and heavy it had to be steered by a smaller one.

The bus station yard was great for roller skating, the timber yard made a fantastic adventure playground and the brick yard provided the means to build houses, fully furnished. **But our favourite game was to build slot machines.** A column of bricks had a tiny peep-hole at the top. This is where the punter dropped their piece of pottery. It fell onto an inverted 'V' shaped piece of tin. We could adjust the position of the tin to make sure we won every time. We went home with pockets full of old broken pottery and felt like millionaires.

Mischief Night was as scary as it was fun. This was the night before Bonfire Night and no-one's supply of wood was safe. In the darkness, raids were made on each other's log piles while **others stalked the houses setting off bull roars and rattling windows.** When we were kids, rainfall pipes were made of cast iron. We stuffed paper up the pipe and set fire to it. The noise it made was splendid. We ran like hell.

We rattled windows by cutting jagged edges into the rims of wooden cotton reels, threading a piece of string through the hole, then running it up and down a window. Another trick was to tie two doors together with rope, knock on each

Forget Tarzan - here's Jen White on the swing (Tears)

door simultaneously and step back to watch the tug of war as each neighbour pulled the other's door shut.

Carol-singing came as a godsend. People were very generous. Even though we often went to the same house night after night, they still found a copper or two for us to share no matter how skint they were. The money was useful for buying small presents for our family. Treats were better though because we could eat them! We sang to a lady who lived opposite the cinema at Darton. We knew her as Miss Fountain and she always gave us sixpence.

Jean Jones, nee Rhodes, says she can laik art...

Bricks were stored in between our gardens and the fields beyond. We built houses. During hay-making, we played in the fields above the brick yard until called in by our mother for bed or chased off by the farmer.

October half-term was for potato-picking. We walked to Moorhouse Farm with our buckets. Joyce Tear was in charge, quite a hard task-master as she shouted, "Heads down, arses up!"

During the long summer holidays, we would spend the whole day in dens in the wood with a good supply of jam sarnies and a little bottle of diluted clinic orange juice. **There was always a baby in the family so we got free orange juice** from the clinic in Darton.

Three or four buses took a children's outing to Scarborough. We were all given a bag of toffee which congealed in our hot, sweaty, little palms. By the time we reached Scarborough, the buses looked as if they had frosted windows with all the sticky finger marks all over them. **Our mam made us throw our toffee into the sea.**

Barnsley Feast Week in August was a great annual occasion. The pits closed and a lot of villagers went to Darton train station to catch the train to Blackpool. They stayed in adjoining streets, in boarding houses, **on a 'room and cruet' basis.** The family brought the food each day and the landlady cooked the food. On the beach, parents sat in a big circle, in deckchairs, with the kids playing safely in the middle.

I'm only little but can I laik sez Phil Crossley...?

Woolley Colliery was completely surrounded by fields and woods which **became the playground for whichever Wild West or wartime battlefield** was being fantasised and fought on that particular day.

Some of our 'playgrounds' we inherited from our forebears, like the swing at 'the Big Dipper'. Then there were the dens made in the woods and the log yard at the pit. There was **riding in the buckets of the aerial flight** as they slowly made their way up and over the pit and stack towards Haigh. There was trekking through the pit sidings and muck stack to make our way to t'Dyke.

Summer time also meant that the pit ponies were brought out from the pit for a two-week break and some of the kids would even ride them bareback up to the fields where they were to be rested and pastured whilst the pit was closed. Something I never did. Too daunting for me! **Those ponies were too wild.**

Spring, summer and autumn were times for collecting **bluebells, hazelnuts, berries and conkers** and it became part of our childhood to be involved as the seasons rolled on. We raided the gardens of the old Top Row for rhubarb, and armed with our sugar wrapped in newspaper, we enjoyed 'our prior to colic' feast. Then would come the raids on Brooke's'orchard on the unmade rough track now called Bloomhouse Lane. **The apples were always cringingly, mouth wateringly sour,** but in fact tasted especially sweet from the victory of not being caught.

In winter we had the 'joy' of slowly freezing, day and night, as the houses were only heated by coal fires. **Icicles nearly three feet long hung from the guttering** and the outside toilet was the

Jen White and Judy Tear put the tail on the donkey
(Tears)

Judy at Blackpool with Jen White
(Tears)

The gang with Bluebell Road in the background
(Browns)

Joyce Brown with Michael Brown, Carol Tickhill, Steven and David Hirst and Philip Crossley going for a walk up Wood-side
(Browns)

The gang's all here again - this time at the back of 7 Bluebell Road, with baby Susan Brown, and Jacqueline Simons, *far right, front row*
(Browns)

last place you wanted to visit. Yet we gladly endured the bitter cold, using old socks for gloves whilst sledging either down the wood path onto Bluebell Road, down the hill from the school to the 'stute or down the school hill and shooting off and over a three foot drop onto the road just outside Mathieson's (now the last house at the top of the Top Row).

It was there that Glen Travis burst his nose against their gatepost because he didn't turn his sledge quick enough when he shot over the drop. **Rough and hardy? Yes,** and the fond memories linger on. Memories like the big sledge made at the pit by the late Kenny Morton and how nearly every kid used it to sledge down the wood path from Brick Row to the bottom of the bus station. Where did that big sledge go? **Keith Wainwright says he still possesses the little sledge that steered the big sledge.** It must be more than 40 years old!

Our Mick and his friends went to the raft pond. There was a crowd of them, Mick Brown, Mick Sanger, Dave Taylor to name a few, and also Ronnie Hunter, **dressed in his mother's lisle stockings to keep warm.** They all took it in turns to jump onto the raft. As each one jumped it moved further out into the pond. By the time it came to Ronnie's turn the raft was quite far out - **he jumped and missed, tore his mum's stockings** and got wet through. Apparently she wasn't very pleased. I don't think he was allowed to play with them again.

Betty Lyman, nee Coatesworth, says she'll laik but don't mess with her...

We used to play in the wood on the Big Dipper as we called it. Once I climbed up to the top of the railings and jumped off. **My foot caught the top railing and I began to spin very fast.** I had to jump off the other side or I would have landed in the tree.

I hit the ground with a right bang - it hurt like hell. Gordon Garforth started laughing at me **so I had to give him a clout,** but I climbed back up and did it again. Nobody would get on the swing if Laddie Whittaker was there, this dog used to jump up and try to bite everyone.

Some of the skipping games were - jelly on a plate, Nebuchadnezzar the King of the Jews, PK penny packet, **on the mountain stands a lady,** Dr McKenzie is a good man, no leaving this rope empty, I went to London in a cockle shell, and many more.

Mr Mills, headmaster, wants to join in...

When I arrived as a temporary headmaster, it was like stepping back in time.

The surrounding woodland fascinated me with its variety of trees, birds and flowers. **One visiting teacher was very excited to find a flower that her reference books said was extinct.** I loved the wildlife, the newt ponds and the ferns but most of all the population. They all cast a spell on me. By the time that the Education Authority decided to continue supporting the school, I was hooked. I couldn't leave.

Autumn Term always started with tearful mothers going home and the new wide-eyed children settling in with friends. We made blackberry jam from the numerous bushes and enjoyed hazelnuts picked straight from the trees. Next was the excitement of bonfire night quickly followed by the rehearsals for the Nativity play. **Every child had a part and all received a present from Santa.**

Spring-time sometimes brought snow. Then it was a magical wonderland! The children would never think of using it as an excuse to stay at home. They would arrive rosy-cheeked dragging their little sledges or plastic bags. Snowmen would be made, snowball fights fought but best of all was the sledging. **The little old stack was as good as the Cresta Run** and the slope down beside the path to the houses was a lovely long ride. **My wife was not best pleased when I arrived home one night with a big tear in my trousers and blood running down my leg** because my sledge had hit a hidden object and my weight had carried me forward onto a nail.

On Pancake Day every child had a piece garnished with sugar, syrup or fruit-juice.

Sports Day was always the highlight of the summer term with flat races, obstacle races, three-legged races and skipping races. If we were blessed with a spell of hot weather lessons were moved outdoors.

One of the innovations of my time was a climbing frame. One child showed me how she enjoyed swinging on the top bar. From a distance, I admired her skills until she gave me the fright of my life. She lost her grip, flew through the air and landed flat on her back on the Tarmac. She lay there shivering but thankfully still alive. Not only alive, but not a single scratch on her. It was a miracle, a magical miracle. Surely she should have a severe injury. Miss Shaw's invisible elves of the woods must have caught her and protected her.

And Terry Taylor wishes he could still laik art...

Woolley Colliery was a dead end for traffic. **I suppose you could say we were the original dead-end kids,** but where the traffic stopped the playground began.

There would be 20 to 30 buses bringing the miners from all around Barnsley, starting to arrive an hour before the start of every shift. The drivers and conductors went to the pit canteen for an hour until the previous shift were ready to be taken home.

When they were parked up and empty those buses, we played hide and seek on them, went round ringing all the bells, **looking under the seats to see if anyone had dropped any coins.** We even tried to get into the drivers' cabs.

One day some bigger lads released the brakes off wagons on the pit sidings and let them go until they completely blocked the road. Then they clamped the brakes back on and stopped all the buses coming in. **All hell broke loose.** How no-one ever got seriously hurt playing in those wagons I will never know.

Of course we argued and fought. We got black eyes and busted noses but it was always one to one, no gang fighting. We played the most foolish and dangerous games in the woods and fields with **spears, catapults, bows and arrows, slings, throwing arrows,** all made ourselves from the facilities around us.

One day when I was seven or eight my brother Dave was brought through the door. My mum screamed, "Oh my God, what's he done?!". "It's alright Gwen" ,this bloke said, "we need to get him to hospital - we think he's broke his arm". Dave had to have a pot on each arm. He had broken them both, **climbing over a 10 foot fence when it collapsed** and he went headlong onto the road.

One winter Sunday afternoon we were all sledging down the causeway on Bluebell Road. Mrs Garforth kept coming up and asking us to move. I had gone up to the top and started my descent on my sledge. I was zooming down when **she suddenly appeared and threw ashes on the sledge track.**

Then she just stood there, legs akimbo, hands on hips, shouting for me to stop. **I looked up and I was terrified.** I lost total control of the sledge, spun round what seemed to be a million times and the next thing her legs went flying in the air. **She landed straight on top of me, almost crushing me,** ooh! she was a big lady.

The sledge was completely flattened and then when we both finally got up she was shouting at everyone as they were quickly dispersing and disappearing into their houses. Then I was on my own, dragging this broken sledge behind me, **crying and carrying one of the runners that had broken off.** I had borrowed this sledge off my mate Maurice Lomas... now I had to explain to him how it got broke, and then I had to go home and explain everything to mum. **Oh heck!**

Easter blessings - *from left*, Unknown, Myra Ashworth, Terry Taylor, Molly Swift, Malc Rhodes, Eugene Senior, Anita Crossley and Jack Joyner
(Coatesworths)

Mavis Ward, Doreen Wraithmell and Heather Senior in front of the outside toilets on the old Top Row
(Wraithmells)

Angels at the Nativity - including Judy Tear, Doreen Wraithmell, *in the middle*, Jen White and Marion Coatesworth
(Wraithmells)

The sledging run from the school down the main road
(Boggs)

Banjo Mamma (Olive) and The Crossley Brothers
(Crossleys)

Chapter Three
T'Stute

Everything happened here once - but all that remains are bits of wood

Just say the words 'Woolley 'Stute' to anyone within two miles of Woolley Colliery and over the age of 60 and you will be rewarded with an all-knowing nod and smug smile as they fondly recall happy times spent there dancing, partying, training, learning or simply meeting.

The need for a community centre was never more evident than during the 1926 General Strike. The school provided breakfasts for the children but they had to make the long trek to the 'Bullet' (Ex-Servicemen's Club) in Darton for a dinner-time bowl of soup.

It was not until more than 10 years later and just before the beginning of the Second World War, that Woolley Colliery finally possessed the centre it richly deserved, being so isolated and with most of its population virtually living in the pit yard.

…materials to build the institute were supplied by Sir William Sutherland, hence its name, the Sutherland Institute, but the actual building work was carried out by the villagers and men from the pit.
Mr and Mrs Tovey

It is probable that the locals, in their excitement and gratitude, took on fund-raising to provide extras in the form of raffles and jumble sales. Or was the Miners' Welfare Fund responsible for its existence?

…this fund was set up in 1920 when a levy of one penny per ton of coal mined was paid into the fund to provide institutes with libraries and reading rooms, sports grounds and parks.
Jean Jones, nee Rhodes

…the 'stute was built in 1939 for the good of the village.
Kathleen Blackburn, nee Crossley

The Sutherland Institute nestled on the hillside above the Top Row. It is remarkable that this green wooden building was destined to be the heart of the community for the next 30 years and it truly was 'good for the village' in a multitude of ways.

…I remember playing on the site as it was being built. After it was finished we used to play underneath it, got in by way of a door I think.
Marjory Whitehead, nee Child

… it was run by a committee of trustees,including Mrs Loft (the manager's wife who lived in the 'big house'.
Mr and Mrs Tovey

They organised the letting, provided crockery and cutlery for functions, employed cleaners, caretakers, fuel deliveries and supervised general maintenance. The T- shaped building was in

regular use for jumble sales, tea dances, whist drives and celebratory parties and its kitchen was a hive of activity, all voluntarily and generously manned.

You could vote in the local and national elections there. Quieter and smaller rooms behind the billiard rooms were used for trustee and Parish Council meetings.

The Second World War endorsed its importance in the village when the trustees rallied to the need of the members of the armed forces by introducing a comforts fund.

…during the war, a group of us would meet to do knitting for the troops. We also made a variety of goods to get money for the funds. One was a vase of flowers made out of a tin can, cut down into strips (dangerous) but not quite down to the base. Then the strips would be shaped and a flower made out of crepe paper stuck on the end.
Marjory Whitehead, nee Child

…when they came home on leave, they received chocolate, cigarettes, gloves, scarf and a choice of hat or helmet.
Mr and Mrs Tovey

…most of the Crossleys and the villagers were at the big party at the end of the war. What a happy picture that was!
Kathleen Blackburn, nee Crossley

…I remember watching this from my bedroom window. There were celebrations in Mrs Pendlebury's backyard. A piano was being played and Mrs Crossley was dancing on an upturned peggy tub.
Jean Jones, nee Rhodes

The local school, having no hall, yet being expected to provide meals for children was also taking more and more advantage of the new facility. The institute took on the role of dining room. At first the dinners were:-

…delivered by horse and cart, and the caretaker was my mam, Mrs Mildred Booth. She did the cleaning up.
Granville Booth

…delivered by Mr Hagen from the kitchens at Darton School and served by Mrs Rene Joyner, Mrs Spurr and Florrie England. We had our own little bottles of brown sauce.
Bob Hudson

…she doled out the slices of meat between a thumb and fore-finger. No-one objected.
Don Rhodes

…his name was Pappy Hagen and his horse was called Seth. It was a horse that was found to be unsuitable for working in the pit so it was sold to him. It was white.
Dave Bogg

The Institute, the heart of the community (Taylors)

Woolley Colliery - *Ar it woh*

...the meals were brought over the fields from Darton, where they were cooked, in big silver-coloured metal containers by horse and cart. Several tables were set out with benches to sit on. Your dinner was served through a hatch. The teachers sat at the head of their year and everybody always wanted to sit next to the teacher but only the chosen few ever did. It caused a lot of jealousy.

Joyce Parling, nee Brown

...I loved the juicy cabbage but the smell of ginger pudding made me feel sick.

Olive Whittles, nee Brown

...later, the dinners were delivered on a coal lorry. Can you imagine that being allowed today?

Billy Crossley

The Government had taken control from the mine owners (Fountain and Burnley) during the Second World War. In 1943, Ernest Bevin demanded that one in 10 conscripts be assigned to work in the mines instead of fighting. Unfortunately, many of them had no experience of pit work. Their selection had been done randomly by ballot using their registration numbers. These recruits were known as Bevin Boys and many of those selected thought themselves unlucky!

As you would expect, the 'stute played its part:-

...the underneath was eventually turned into a mock mining gallery for trainees. In the rooms above, young miners attended classes which included first aid and fire-fighting.

Billy Crossley

...Walter Booth was the first aid man, he was the ambulance man at the pit.

Olive Whittles, nee Brown

...but it was Tommy Ward who taught first aid to the new recruits.

Dave Bogg

...we used him as our local doctor, treating sprains, bruises and minor injuries.

Joyce Parling, nee Brown

...Freddy Crowther was a pit fire-fighter (fireman). All the fire-fighters had Fireman nameplates on the wall outside their respective houses. He was also the boiler-house man for the 'stute and tended the coal-fired boiler for years.

Billy Crossley

The war ended but the community spirit lived on and thrived as the 'stute continued to be the heart of the village's social life and school activities.

...the bonfire outside number 13 denoted the end of the Second World War. I had started school by then (in 1943). The headmaster was Mr Wittingstall, Standards 1 and 2 were taught by Miss Coy and for the primary class, it was Miss Shaw.

Dave Bogg

Children were marched down in crocodile-style for country dancing and physical education.

...when I was about eight, we started having Music and Mime with Mrs Leigh. This was a radio programme from the B.B.C. We had to be trees or mountains.

Joyce Parling, nee Brown

The new headmaster was Mr Geldard and he ran confirmation classes.

...several of us attended, all girls. We had to wear white when we were confirmed. All the time we were having these night-time classes, the grinning faces of Geoff Ward and David Tear looked through the windows and pulled faces at us.

Joyce Parling, nee Brown

...I remember going to Royston for some confirmation classes. I think we were confirmed there. It suited me because the lads were better-looking in Royston.

Jen James, nee White

Even the outside of the 'stute served a purpose: -

...we held concerts on the steps, dressed in old bridesmaid dresses, singing and dancing and using all our imagination.

Joyce Parling, nee Brown

...as a kid I remember we used to pester my mum to let us go for a picnic. So with sandwiches and a bottle of water we set off with no idea of where we were going to go. However, we always ended up on the 'stute steps, tucking in even though we'd had our dinner only an hour before.

Olive Whittles, nee Brown

Concerts were organised to celebrate Easter with bonnet parades, Christmas nativities and New Year fancy dress parties. And the highlight of the evening?: -

...row after row of plates, each holding two curling sandwiches, a chocolate marshmallow, a lemon curd tart and a fairy bun awaited collection in the interval. A fantastic treat all on one plate! All prepared and served by Eva Senior, Mrs Rhodes and Daisy Turner with a cup of tea.

Judy Speight, nee Tear

...Christmas was a magical time, with a village party and dance always being held in the Sutherland Institute. Games for the kids, as well as grown-ups, were played and enjoyed during the evening. Food seemed plentiful and drink flowed (for kids, Beckett's limeade or dandelion and burdock pop, with packets of crinkly XL crisps to eat) and then dancing took over as the night progressed.

Phillip Crossley

...there were fancy dress competitions. One year when it was raining, I went as Little Boy Blue but being wet and squashed in the 'stute, my outfit disintegrated and the tissue paper dyed my skin blue.

Joyce Parling, nee Brown

Betty Tear, nee Bird, the dancing teacher who held classes at the 'stute
(Tears)

Lads at play
(Boggs)

Fireman who trained at the 'stute, from *back row, left,* Johnny Caves, Jack Bannister, Wilfred Rhodes, Dennis Ward, *middle row, from left,* Frank Booth, Freddie Crowther, 'Bacchus' Wraithmell, Colin Senior, Kenny Morton, *bottom row, from left,* Ken Turner, Morris Lumb
(Wraithmells)

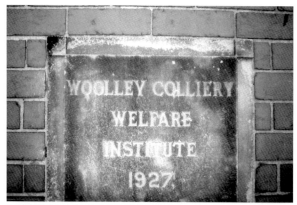

Commemorative stones still to be found at the Woolley Welfare
(Browns)

The day-trippers - setting off in for an outing in 1920s, and just look at those hats!
(Boggs)

Delegates' day out to the seaside - a trip from Woolley, including Joe Burbridge, *far left*
(Boggs)

Kiss me quick - Woolley folk having fun at Blackpool Pleasure Beach include Joe Burbridge, *top row, second left*
(Boggs)

Woolley Colliery Ambulance Class

Mary had a little Lamb
Jack Horner had a Pie
We have Scented Cards
To sell you—BUY and BUY.
Alexander Fredericks.

Designs & verses, copyright and fully protected under Act 1911 by Fredk. Brown, Manufacturer, Wormgate Printing Works, BOSTON England.

Just the ticket - fund-raising for the Ambulance Class
(Tears)

The Welfare at Woolley Colliery - another meeting place for the community
(Boggs)

...my cousin David (Tear) and I celebrated V.J. Day, getting married, at a fancy dress party and won first prize I think. It's a good job somebody took a photo because I can't remember anything, not even getting dressed for it!

Jen James, nee White

...Saturday morning dance classes with tap and ballet were held, instructed by Betty Bird (Tear), culminating in a concert.

Jean Jones, nee Rhodes

...I was dressed as a fairy in a concert during the 1940s. We did a balloon dance as part of a group. Jean Crowther was the head fairy, singing, 'When you wish upon a star'. Freddie, Jean's dad, fixed a battery to her clothes with a wire up her back to a star on her head which would light up.

Jenny Hepworth, nee Hudson

...it was a three act play followed by the class showing off their dancing skills. In the first act me and my 'brother' Alfie Waller, who was an evacuee and lived at Mrs Senior's, New Top Row, with his sister, were being cared for by our nurse played by Brenda England . When we went to bed, I had a dream, Jean Crowther waved a wand over me and sang 'When you wish upon a star'. In the next act, Alfie and I were in Fairyland, Sheila Loft was the Queen with all the fairies dancing for us. I sang a song for them. In the final scene we were back in our beds with nurse getting cross with us for sleeping late. It was a really good show and all good fun.

Marjory Whitehead, nee Child

Carnival Queens were chosen, attendants watched jealously and pageboys winced at the thought of the part they had to play:-

...the Gala Queen was picked in the 'stute, and the night our Marion was picked we were all there as usual. Some 'big noises' were there too, probably the Lord Mayor and Lady Mayoress.
  Someone opened the window and shouted, "It's Marion Coatesworth who's been picked, ay up Pat, it's your Mario!".
  I was thrilled to bits. She had looked so lovely in her yellow frock and red shoes, and her black hair. I flew across the field, round Mathiesons' corner, and up Bluebell Road to tell our lot at home that our Marion was going to be Gala Queen.

Mavis Tomalic, nee Coatesworth

...there was a carnival every year in the summer when a girl was picked from the village to be Carnival Queen. This was done in the 'stute where all the girls had to walk round so the pit manager and his wife could choose. One year I was chosen to be attendant to Marion Coatesworth. Pauline Hughes lent me a blue bridesmaid dress of hers and I felt like a queen. I'd never worn a long dress before.

Joyce Parling, nee Brown

...I was up for pageboy but lost out to Jackie Waller. I know why. My parents couldn't or wouldn't pay for the costume.

Dennis Crossley

...I was an attendant with Pauline Joyner when Irene Sacre was May Queen. Billy Crossley and Jackie Waller were page boys. Arthur Greenwood M.P. presented a five shilling crown to all on parade.

Jen James, nee White

...we used to ride round the village on the back of a decorated coal lorry and end up on the sports field, opposite the Welfare, and have a sports day. But if it rained we had the carnival in the 'stute. It seemed to be very crowded.

Joyce Parling, nee Brown

Beetle drives, concerts, plays and faith suppers, often followed by dancing, filled dismal evenings before television was affordable to most mining families: -

...and as we were too young or too poor to go to them, we spent hours peering through the windows in wonder at these events.

Olive Whittles, nee Brown

And one of many ways of recycling, before recycling was a necessity rather than a virtue:-

...jumble sales were held at the 'stute and at the end, any old coats not sold were taken by Grandma Crossley to make into clippie or rag rugs. She set us on (grandchildren) cutting them into strips, elongated diamond clippings, with shears not scissors. A large, long piece of hessian material was stretched and rolled across a wooden frame and with a metal brodder or a sharpened peg, clippings were broddled through the hessian. Sometimes a pattern of diamonds, squares or circles would be drawn on the hessian and broddled in separate colours. What luxury to walk on!

Joyce Parling, nee Brown

...winter was the time to 'brod' a new rug. There was no wall-to-wall carpets, just oil-cloth or at best, a couple of coconut mats.

Dave Bogg

Young men paid their annual subscription of half a crown to George Turner, a trustee, for use of the snooker/billiards tables, dartboard and cards. Another great favourite was Kenny Morton's keep fit, gymnastics and boxing classes which he ran in the early 1950s. Many, many people recalled these activities so they were obviously popular:-

...he (Kenny Morton) was assisted by Terry Joyner, Johnny Caves, Henry Foster, Gerald Foster, Roy Bottomley and me.

Bob Hudson

But the most well-remembered activity was the Friday night dances. Everyone contributing to this book seems to have their own special memory. Teenagers, or younger, from the outlying villages of Darton, Kexborough, Barugh and Staincross walked or caught Cawthorne's bus to Woolley Colliery to join their school friends and families:-

The infamous Cawthorne Bomber - vital transport to the 'stute dances
(Boggs)

Sweet little rock'n'rollers, Margaret Empsall and Joyce Brown
(Empsalls)

Queen for the day - Irene Sacre, the 1952 Carnival Queen, attended by Jen White, Jackie Waller, Pauline Joyner and Pauline Hughes
(Tears)

Ernest Crossley and Mrs Croft with Jen White and Jackie Waller
(Tears)

Choirmaster Mr Walton and his songbirds - *top row, from left*, Dennis Crossley, Billy Crossley, David Sanger, Doreen Wraithmell, Mavis Coatesworth, Mary Bogg; *middle row, from left*, Jen White, Pat Chadwick, Doreen Sanger, Betty Coatesworth, Tony Mathieson, Jack Joyner, Alan Bogg, Eugene Senior, Jeff Sacre; *bottom row, from left*, Lilian Swift, Valerie Lockwood, Pauline Hughes, Marion Coatesworth, Joyce Brown, Stuart Rhodes, Alec Richardson
(Coatesworths/Wraithmells)

Dancing the Gay Gordons at the Easter fancy dress party at the 'stute
(Unknown)

Jen White and David Tear celebrating V.J. Day at the bottom of Fountain Square
(Tears)

…it was known as the Bob Hop because it cost a shilling to get in.

Dave Bogg

George Turner and Mrs Allott taught old-time and sequence dancing to records played on an old gramophone hidden behind a screen. We grabbed any willing partner and copied their steps. Daisy Turner, Edna Booth and Eva Senior sold refreshments during the interval.

…my anxieties began at 4pm on Fridays when my dad gave me my dance money. Half a crown was great but a florin caused problems. The fare on Cawthorne's bus was 2d up and 2d back to the Bullet. The entry fee was a shilling, pop was 6d and crisps 4d. Now anyone can see that this is 2s 2d. However, all was not lost! If my uncle Doug (Senior) was driving the bus, I got a free ride. Or if my Aunty Eva was serving the crisps, she bought them for me. Failing that, I walked home! What a great night!

Judy Speight, nee Tear

…Mrs Rhodes taught me to dance the St. Bernard's waltz, the polly glide, quickstep and waltz before rock and roll took over. I remember Martin Cotton and Flick Lawton bopping and strutting their stuff to Bill Haley and the Comets showing us all how it was done. Mavis Horsley (Bretton) taught me to rock and roll. She sang in a group with Jack Horsley and Peter Garforth.

Dennis Crossley

…my cousin Mick Brown, who worked on the pit top, had a bet that he could get into the dance in his pit muck and buy a bottle of pop. This amused Daisy Turner so much that she let him in.

Billy Crossley

…the Teenage Rebels were Colin Beaumont (piano), Jimmy Naylor (trumpet), Les Telfer (vocals), Pete 'Flick' Lawton (bass), Pete Eagan (drums) and Mavis Bretton (vocals). They were the first rock band to play there. Flick went on to to play with the Trackers, who were Tony Christie's backing band. Barry Tovey, Terry Taylor and I played guitars.

Billy Crossley

Wedding 'do's' hold strong memories, especially as the custom was for the bride's father to throw a handful of pennies into the crowd of clambering, grovelling, dishevelled kids waiting at the steps.

…June 6, 1959 was our wedding reception after a ceremony at Woolley Village church conducted by Rev. Wilby.

Brian and Jen James, nee White

…our wedding reception was in 1959, complete with a sherry toast and H.P. brown sauce on the tables. It was lovely… I think my cousin Catherine's was shortly after mine.

Olive Whittles, nee Brown

…the wedding I remember was Pearl Stables to Eric Holland. Eric picked Pearl up and carried her from the 'stute all the way through the village to her mother's house and over the threshold.

Billy Crossley

…My wedding reception was held there on March 3, 1962. I don't know if there were any more after that. Our do was a ham salad, a monster pile of bread and butter and a trifle from Waggie's (Wilshaw's) in Darton.

Jean Jones, nee Rhodes

Great excitement hit the village again around 1955. Wilfred Pickles and Mabel came to 5 Bluebell Road, to visit Tony Marley. In those days Wilfred Pickles did a 'Fix it/ dreams come true' type of radio programme. Tony wished to meet Derek Dooley who had broken his leg playing football.

…Wilfred fixed it for Tony to meet Derek. I think Jen James got his autograph. I saw it all from my bedroom window.

Billy Crossley

…Tony lived next door to us in Bluebell Road. He asked to meet Derek Dooley who played for Sheffield Wednesday, and had lost a leg through gangrene.'The Barnsley Chronicle' took photos.

Joyce Parling, nee Brown

…he came as part of a magazine 'Dreams Come True' feature and called at the home of Tommy and Dora Waller (Tony Marley's mother). He was accompanied by Violet Carson (Ena Sharples of 'Coronation Street') I think. She played the piano on his show 'Have a Go Joe'. Everyone was sworn to secrecy otherwise it would have been cancelled. Wilfred was a smoker and had his own cigarettes with his autograph on. Even non-smokers accepted cigarettes from him as a souvenir. The story appeared in the magazine a few weeks later.

Jim Hudson

After 1962 we have no photos of the 'stute and no mention of any activities so we must assume its demolition took place shortly after that date.

…the village mounted a petition to save the 'stute but because of its bad state of repair and there being no available land (as it was all owned by the NCB by this time) it was impossible to save so it had to be demolished.

Mr and Mrs Tovey

…a group of us tried to raise money by holding pea and pie suppers and dances to keep it open.

Dennis Crossley

…wood from the old institute was put to good use making pigeon lofts, sheds and garden fencing.

Mr and Mrs Tovey

…some of the wood from the demolished building was used to repair Jack Rhodes' hen hut up Sackup Lane, Bloomhouse. It's still standing.

Jean Jones, nee Rhodes

Close-up of the happy couple - salad teas all round
(Rhodes)

Wedding belle - the 1962 reception of Jean, nee Rhodes, and Peter Jones, with their parents, in the 'stute
(Rhodes)

Anybody for H.P. sauce? - the wedding reception of Olive Brown and Roy Whittles at the 'stute in 1959
(Browns)

Friends on an outing to the next village - *from left*, Olive Brown, Mrs Ellis, Mr Ellis, Walter Brown, Lionel (second name unknown), Jack Empsall, Hilda Brown, Milly Brown, Grandma Brown, Great Aunt Dora and Jim Brown
(Browns)

Jack Rhodes mending his pigeon loft with wood from the demolished 'stute
(Rhodes)

OUR PERSONAL STORIES

Everybody's memories are special. There were so many wonderful ones we had to share some of them with you in full...

Elizabeth Coatesworth, nee Wiles, written in 1999 - To serve them all my days

I was born at Brick Row on June 22, 1917, to Sarah and Lewis Wiles. I had two older sisters Gladys and Ruth, and Sam Joyner, my cousin, always lived with us. We got on well me and **our Sam, he was better than a brother to me.**

A young Elizabeth Coatesworth
(Coatesworths)

On Saturdays I had to clean cutlery with Brasso and emery paper and also clean all the boots and shoes ready for Sunday. Then **me and our Sam had to scrub the cellar steps.** We hated it as there were spiders and creepy-crawlies!

We used to get a Saturday penny and take it on to Lister's shop up High Street to spend. Sometimes we only got a halfpenny depending on the financial state. My friend Lily Sands and I used to buy a stick of hard liquorice, fill up a medicine bottle with water, cut the Spanish up into it and swish it round. We would sit on the garden seat and make it last all day.

On Sundays we had to go to church twice, mornings and afternoons, even three times if it was a special service. In summer we would go a walk after all that, to the O'er Tops and fetch a bottle of spring water; as Mother said, it made a lovely cup of tea.

There was no water on tap, we had to fetch it from the row end, before school. Sometimes in summer the water was off so we had to trail up Farmers' hill and onto Beamshire wood, to the O'er Tops for the spring water.

At home, for drinking water we had a large earthenware container, and used a ladling can to get it. Outside **we collected rainwater in tubs.** The night before washday Dad took the wooden square that held two big buckets and filled the set-pot. The fire underneath was lit so the water would be hot ready for the early morning start of washday.

Clothes had to be soaked in a tub, rubbed on the rubbing board then scrubbed on the table before rinsing could begin. Whites were boiled in the set-pot. A lot of starch and dolly blue were used, but **mainly it was elbow grease that shifted the muck!** Once the washing was done the hot water was used to scrub anything wooden. Then the stone-flagged floor was scrubbed, next the steps and finally the flags were swilled. Water was never wasted.

On Saturday nights Barnsley Market stayed open late and **Mam often shopped at 9pm.** She got a cheap joint of meat and all kinds of fruit and vegetables - they nearly gave them away!

We all had to run errands but never expected paying for it. My friend Mary and I used to go up to the farm for taties and turnips. Sometimes we would watch the cowman milking; it was all done by hand then. In the summertime the farmer's wife would let us pick gooseberries and redcurrants. Later, **she let us have windfalls of apples and pears.**

There was a Carnival every year down in Mapplewell village. There were all kinds of floats and folks in fancy dress. There was fun and games for the kids' races with prizes. **They roasted a bull,** it was there for all to see, then folks could buy a beef sandwich.

On Saturdays some of the Brick Row kids went to the 'Penny Rush' down at the Picture House, some took jam jars to pay. But **I never saw a film until I was working, in service.**

Home coals were tipped near the flags then shovelled down the grating into the cellar. There was always a lot of slack or small coal in a load so the fire could be made up and damped down to stay in allnight, it only needed riddling in the morning and you had a warm fireside to get dressed by.

The fireplace had to heat the oven and there was a side-pan to heat water. The kettle was kept boiling on the rib. The fireplace was high and open at the front. There was a grid on which Mother let down a flap to put flat irons on to heat up for the ironing. The mantelpiece was high and a long shelf went the length of the range to keep food hot. There was a length of cord on which we dried small things like socks or tea towels. We had a fender and a tidy betty in front.

There were no pithead baths so **dad had to bath at home in front of the fire** in a zinc tub. All us kids had our bath Saturday night. Sometimes we had milk pobs or Oxo after a hot bath. There was no electricity; we had paraffin lamps for light and Kelly lamps or candles to take up to bed at night.

Everybody had paper blinds which they pulled down at night; they cost about 6d each.

You could buy wallpaper for 2 ½ d a roll, but had to trim all the edges. Flour and water was the usual paste. You could buy a block of salt nearly a yard long for a few coppers.

Dad taught us dominoes and several card games. He gave us two old pennies when we managed to recite the alphabet backwards. **Dad was partial to Blue Boy toffee** and often gave us some while we played cards.

We had to do a lot of darning, socks or the elbows of cardigans as we couldn't afford new often. **We had to wait our turn for new boots,** and they had to be mended at least three times before being thrown out or used to light the fire.

We had a rug frame on which dad nailed harding. We used to all work on the rug but dad did the most. While we pegged away mam would be working on her quilt. She used to buy 1d packets of Dolly Rags, some were very pretty patterns and they brightened up your quilts, making them very smart and stylish. Then **we'd have roasters and beef dripping with red cabbage for supper.**

Everybody made their own bread. Mam always did a stone at a time in a great big pansion. You used to feel hungry when you smelled it baking, it was the same on Sundays as the roast beef and Yorkshire puddings cooked, your mouth fair watered! **She usually made eight loaves at a time,** sometimes oven bottom cakes for a change. She also made lovely spice cake as well.

In summer we went blackberry picking. Mam could make jam faster than we could pick. She also made nettle beer and the corks sometimes blew after she had bottled it. **She always had some sort of herb tea on the go** like peppermint or camomile. Mam also made elderberry syrup which we were given to ward off the colds. If we were off it, she would wrap the oven shelf in an old cloth to keep us warm in bed.

Everybody used to keep their windows nice and clean, and also scoured their steps with donkey stone and kept their flags swept. **There were no flush toilets; they were earth closets** which we had to share with our neighbours. Ashes and other rubbish went behind the midden. No toilet rolls, newspaper was cut into squares. The night man came with his horse and cart, once a week to clear them out. Phew, what a rotten job!

The soil was good in our garden and dad was able to grow most vegetables, also herbs, rhubarb and an array of flowers. We kept poultry down the bottom of the garden so had plenty of fresh eggs.

We had two rabbits which we fed on oats and tea-leaves in winter and carrots and rabbit meat (dandelions) from up the farmer's hill in summer. We also had a ginger cat that liked the garden better than the house, it was a good mouser!

Marion Brackin, nee Coatesworth - Want owt from t'Colliery shop?

Father Lawrence, mother Elizabeth nee Wiles, brothers and sisters Joan, Lewis, Marion, Betty, Mavis, Patricia and Sheila... Our family were all born and lived at Brick Row in a back-to-back-house, which consisted of an attic, bedroom, living room-cum-kitchen and a cellar with a well in it. **The toilet was a midden across the street** shared with our neighbours.

In 1948 we were told we were moving to Woolley Colliery. We attended Woolley Colliery School and the church and knew most of the children who lived there. But to be going into a new house with three bedrooms plus bathroom and two toilets was a luxury; we also had a wash-house with an electric boiler for the clothes. We moved in August to 12 Bluebell Road and I lived there until I got married on June 3, 1961.

Many Colliery folk kept hens, we did, so did Garforths, only theirs were bantams. Rabbits were popular, also polecats among the poaching fraternity. The last people I remember keeping pigs were Mr and Mrs Gosling. Bluey was a stocky, dapper man who always sported a flower in his buttonhole, he was a keen crown green bowler and enjoyed being out and about, **his only downside was he chewed baccy and spat a lot.** Dora Gosling (Aunty Dora) was small and plump, in a cross-over pinny. She was always at home. You took your peelings and scraps to her for the pigs, and she gave you a twist of spice, Yorkshire mixtures or dolly mixtures.

The old shop on the Top Row, familiar to all in Woolley Colliery
(Crossleys)

We always had two tabby cats, they fended for themselves, no cat food, only milk and bacon swads. Eva Jump had a tortoise and an old dog called Bruce. **Dogs roamed freely round the Colliery streets,** these were Buddy Bogg, Dusty Crossley and a nasty one, Laddie Whittaker. Our Lewis mated with Alan Bogg and Buddy was part of their gang.

Lots of miners were pigeon fanciers, Sangers and Hunters in particular, on our side of Bluebell Road. When a race was on the men would gather at their lofts, eyes scanning the skyline.

Someone would spot a lone bird and they'd start shaking the tins of corn, 'Come in - come in' to encourage their birds home. Sometimes they'd cheer in triumph, knowing they could have won, often, **there would be curses of frustration as their pigeons landed on rooftops,** fluttering about, refusing to 'come in' to be checked.

Cars were a rare sight at the Colliery in the 1950s. There was only Travis's taxis on the old Top Row, and Mr Connor from Bluebell Road, a boss at the laboratories, had a little black car.

Scrace and Dunford's cart came on Friday nights, fruit and veg, and liquorice sticks, the natural kind, you could chew them for hours. Various butchers' carts came, **a pot and pan man came on Friday afternoon.** Sometimes a little old man selling haberdashery out of a suitcase came on a Saturday. Mam always found a few coppers to buy buttons or reels of cotton, but nowt spare for hair ribbons.

Then we'd get the gypsies. **Mam was scared of being cursed,** and always bought their pegs or lavender bags. Sometimes 'Holy Joes' would preach on the door step, but dad could spout all the Bible passages back at them, so they would give up and clear off eventually.

Marion Coatesworth and Pete Brackin - 18 going on 48
(Coatesworths)

The Colliery shop was run by Cyril Burrows and his wife Connie. Wendy Mathieson also had a spell working there. I got my first pocket money by 'shopping' for all the old folks. You got thrupence for a quick nip on the Top Row, but **going down to Darton was an expedition involving borrowing dad's bike,** so that was at least a tanner.

I adored dad's bike, I used to ride it, legs through the cross-bar, getting greased-up socks from the chain. He used to send me down to the low canteen, early mornings, for his Craven A. One day I lost the money in the snow, so dad got no fags. I kept out of his way for days. Another time, **I was dolly-daydreaming and lost a ten bob note,** somewhere on the Top Row. I knew mam's shopping list by heart: two loaves uncut bread, ¼ potted beef, Dairylea cheeses, packet of Korays (pink aspirin) and ¼ Mintoes. I knew Mintoes weighed 13 sweets to a quarter, I always took 12 home, (one sucked *en route*).

I was appalled at losing that ten bob note, and was nearly home, in tears, when either Philip or Dennis Crossley (who had seen me searching) called me in to see Mr Crossley. He seemed very stern (to me), questioned me at length, then produced the ten bob note, telling me to be more careful in future. Phew, what a relief.

Once when I was shopping, buying kayli and Spanish, Wendy Lumb came in and bought a Toblerone. **I was speechless that she could afford such a luxury,** I mean, it was only the pit office girls who bought suchlikes.

In 1953 we were walking down to Darton Picture House to watch the Coronation of Queen Elizabeth II. We were in the front circle! A phenomenon I couldn't get over, upstairs in the Picture House, all I knew was the matinee (matney) on a Saturday (satdy) morning.

Flash Gordon, he always hung over the cliff, but next week was always saved. We were bossed about by a series of monitors, one in particular being 'Umboppa'. Lord knows where he got his name, but he strutted his stuff and his word was law in the Saturday morning matinee.

Some of the big lads helped at hay-making. Summertime we walked over to Moorhouse and Haigh, or down to Woolley Village, to Brickyard at Woolley crossroads, where Auntie Ruth and Uncle Bill lived. He was the shepherd at Rowbottoms' farm. But mostly we stayed home..

In the late 1940s Uncle Benny's son had emigrated to Canada. He went to visit him and brought back an Indian outfit, complete with huge feather headdress. Much to our embarrassment, he used to enter local fancy dress shows in the full regalia, complete with war paint. Needless to say, he won a lot. We were speechless, I mean fancy dress was for children to shine. **Why would an old codger like him enter?**

I remember Sheila Hodgson going as 'Keyhole Kate'. She wore glasses anyway, so played the part to her advantage, I admired her for that. We all called Sheila's mother 'Salome'.

On at the Gala Field at the Woolley Welfare, **there were the Slowest Bicycle Racers,** and the pit fire fighters put on their display of speed and accuracy through imaginary underground tunnels.

Some distant relatives turned up from Lupset near Wakefield, (another planet as far as we were concerned). They went over the fields to our house, **mam sent us after them 'in case they go ferreting about our upstairs',** though God knows we had little enough, never had owt to pinch!

The church played a big part in our lives. We went to Sunday school in the morning and the service at night. Mr Wilby was the vicar and we went to prayer meetings with Miss Dearnley. She was the Sunday school teacher but she made it feel more like a Youth Club than church. **Wednesday evenings we did sewing and games.**

Due to her encouragement I went on to be confirmed, in March 1955, at Royston church by the Lord Bishop of Pontefract. Once we were doing the Christmas story and had to learn it all off by heart. I was an angel and **we had to embroider our wings for weeks on end in long and short stitches.** They were an impressive sight when finished. In the school choir, I always sang *Mary was watching tenderly, her little Son.*

I took over from our Mave as the Walshes' babysitter. They were Muriel and Roy and their children were Gary and Gail. Gary had learning difficulties, he looked perfect, a pretty, fair-haired boy, but he was hard work. Of course 50 years ago there wasn't much done, and the Walshes muddled through as best they could; autism hadn't been diagnosed.

In the summer of 1959, Reg acquired a car, and one day I went with them up the Strines! Well, talk about opening my eyes! I couldn't believe that in under an hour we could be transformed into a world of steep heather-clad hills, with hairpin bends, into water-filled valleys. A paradise. **I realised there was a world outside of Woolley Edge and Darton.**

Betty Lyman, nee Coatesworth - There were nine in the bed

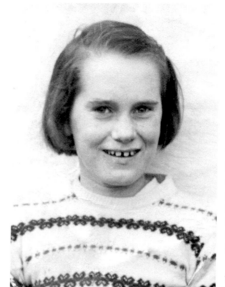

Betty Coatesworth - Queen of the mabs
(Coatesworth)

The first time I heard of Woolley Colliery was when I started school at the age of five, in 1948. **At that time I lived up Brick Row,** which was up through the wood from Woolley Colliery, about half a mile, and consisted of two rows of back-to-back houses. I lived there with my mum, dad, five sisters and one brother.

There were nine of us in one bedroom, we had two beds and a cot, we slept three at the top, three at the bottom and one in the cot. The small room downstairs consisted of a black-leaded fireplace, a set-pot, and a sink. Our furniture was a rocking chair, a table and a dresser. **We had neither gas or electricity.** The toilet was outside across the yard, we called them duckets in the middin and we shared with our next door neighbour.

We moved to Woolley Colliery in summer, into a three-bedroomed house, **it seemed huge compared to the one we had been living in.** Lots of Brick Row families moved at the same time, there were the Sangers, Garforths, Armitages, Sacres, Margisons, Coatesworths (us) and some others.

Ian Geoffrey King - The long road from Suffolk to Woolley

We came to Moorhouse from a small hamlet on Middleton Moor in Suffolk in the early 1950s. **Far Moorhouse was up a long bumpy lane from Haigh,** passing Richmond's farm, then some more houses halfway on, which had a pond at the front of them and I think the Popplewells lived there.

Ian King lived at Moorhouse
(Kings)

Then on the right was Tears' cottage and the Plantings and **finally you came to Moorhouse Farm which consisted of two dwellings.** There was my dad Philip, mum Hilda and brother Malcolm when we moved to Moorhouse.

Our sister Shirley was born at Moorhouse on July 26, 1953 after we had been there about two years. It was Auntie Sylvia who stopped with us until Mum was okay after childbirth as Dad was not able to have time off in those days.

Dad brought us to Yorkshire because **farm labourers' wages were better than in Suffolk** at the time; also there was an added bonus for mum as her sister lived in Barnsley, off Summer Lane. This was Sylvia and her husband Johnny Lingwood - Uncle Johnny worked at Woolley Colliery as machine-man on regular night shift.

Dad was a farm labourer for Richmonds, which involved numerous types of work around the farm; tractor-driving, milking cows, seeding, planting, feeding livestock and harvesting and threshing, that's just to mention but a few.

He could be at work from dawn until dusk some days. If he wasn't at work he would be tending to a large strip of land that Mr Richmond allowed him to cultivate as a garden, growing sufficient root crops to store to help the household budget throughout the year. He also grew all the seasonal vegetables and salad items. He always said hard work never killed anyone! **He even managed rabbits and pheasants for us to devour.**

The house had no electricity, hot water, bathroom or indoor toilet, just a cold water supply. The toilet was a back-to-back midden, one for each of the dwellings. You sprinkled a pink powder down after use. It was then emptied manually onto a collection lorry with shovels.

Washing was a full day's work even when the weather was fine. Tempers were a bit frayed if it was a wet day, with damp washing hung all around. Then after all this it had to be ironed, mum was very fussy. **Every item was ironed, from the smallest hanky to socks** and collars and cuffs on best shirts were starched. God bless mum.

Lighting was provided by paraffin lamps of various types, candles and torches. Heating was by open fire or Aladdin paraffin heaters, sometimes both in the wintertime.

Our next door neighbours at that period were the Nichols Family, Mr and Mrs Nichols, sons Brian, David and daughter Christine. Mr Nichols worked as a railway bobby. The next nearest neighbours were Eddie and Betty Tear, who became good friends of my parents. Their children were David and Heather.

The only entertainment was a radio that ran on an accumulator and battery, with programmes such as *Listen with Mother, Baby Bunting, Henry Hall, Billy Cotton, Mrs Dale's Diary, Dick Barton, The Archers and Forces Favourites.*

Mum had been in service for the gentry prior to marrying dad. She'd learnt to be an excellent cook and baker. She could skin and fillet fish as she was a fishmonger's daughter, pluck a bird, and skin a rabbit faster than anyone I've ever known.

She was also a skilled darner and prolific knitter, which she did in the evenings even when lighting was sparse. Brodding clippie rugs was another chore and this was all we had on the floor besides lino.

A grocery hawker came once a week. His name was Mr Bateson. He would come in a three wheeler van with a motor bike engine. You knew he was coming due to the sound of the engine. Mum got most of her weekly needs from him as it saved her carrying them from Cyril Burrows' shop at Woolley or even further from Darton shops. But of course there was always something Mum had to get from elsewhere such as stamps, postal orders, meat or small items of clothing. So **she would have to either walk to the shop or post office at Haigh,** or if not walk the other way to Darton where there was a good selection of shops.

At least once a fortnight dad had to go for a re-charged accumulator and paraffin from Ellis and Booths' garage, he either walked it with us or balanced them on a push-bike; this was tricky as there was acid in the accumulator and **he managed burn a hole more than once in his clothes.**

Mum bought most of her main clothing and large items from a mail order catalogue, for which she received some meagre commission. She didn't go to Barnsley or Wakefield as there was never enough ready cash to pay outright. **She was a brilliant juggler where money was concerned.**

Whenever we had to have a home visit **Dr Herbert would arrive at Moorhouse on his trusty steed, his bag strapped to the saddle,** Harris tweed jacket on, riding boots and jodhpurs. I think he really looked forward to calls in

Ian King's father Philip - who came to Woolley from Suffolk
(Kings)

our vicinity, so that he could get some riding practice in for when he used to ride with the hounds. He was a very tall formidable man, loud and very jolly.

On one occasion mum had walked to Haigh to a phone to request a home visit, as she suspected scarlet fever and he was at our house not long after mum had returned from phoning the surgery.

He must have been riding his horse like a pony express rider to get there so quick. He confirmed that I had scarlet fever; I must have been upset at the thought of going into hospital. I can remember to this day a smile on his face as he said I'll just have a word with your mother.

They both came back into the bedroom and he said, **"it's your lucky day, we are going to isolate you in this room with nobody to see you,** only your mother until you are better". He actually came back the next day with my medication so that mum did not have to leave me on my own. Then he arranged for a chap to come and fumigate the house.

There was no being mollycoddled by car or bus; we had to walk to school across the fields and through the wood, a distance of a good mile, come rain, snow or blow. It wasn't long before my brother and I had palled up with several of the Colliery lads. I can remember a few, David Toll, Ian Moody, Tiffy Butler, David Haywood, Kenny Hunter and Barry Cooper, plus all the lads from Moorhouse end, Brian and David Nichols, David and Heather Tear, and Martin Richmond.

Hilda King with Ian King on her knee - they had both had their hair done!
(Kings)

The Colliery school had the best playground. It was a wood. It had swings, dens and ideal trees for climbing. We wandered so far into the wood we couldn't hear the bell. A teacher would have to ring it a lot louder and longer.

With dad working at the farm, he got free passes to The Great Yorkshire Show, loaned a car and took us on the final day. On Sundays in the summertime, we would don our Sunday best, including shoes that dad had brayed segs in to make them last longer. Dad wore his suit, tie and trilby. **Mum put her best outfit on and off we'd go, up the track to Woolley Edge,** down Gypsy Lane, around Woolley Village, and back up Middle Field Lane, home just in time for tea.

Holidays were visiting our grandparents and relations in Suffolk, mum had four sisters and five brothers, dad had two brothers and a sister all expecting a visit.

We used to stay at my grandparents and do a tour around the rest, as it would be at least a year before we were able to visit again. **Dad could afford to hire a car because** we were at our grandparents with free lodgings.

Mum and dad had become good friends with Mr and Mrs Tear from just up the lane from Moorhouse. I can remember one year, dad hired a bigger car for the trip down to Suffolk. This was so there would be enough room for our family and Mr and Mrs Tear.

Dad then took a little detour and dropped Eddie and Betty off at Great Yarmouth, and picked them up on the return journey. By doing it this way at that time, they were doing each other a favour, halving the costs of the transport.

In 1955 dad managed to find another job with more pay and better prospects at Felkirk near South Hiendley and we flitted. **Several years later I was brought back into the fold,** as I met Patricia Coatesworth at a dance hall and we were married on April 1, 1967 at Woolley Village Parish Church.

Judy Speight, nee Tear - My very special childhood on the farm...

Grandad Joe was the kindest of people, enjoyed the simple pleasures in life and thought only good of people. He was contented and happy with his lot. **He had a permanent smile.**

His patience was endless. He lifted us, his grandchildren, onto the backs of the plough horses and walked us tirelessly around the farmyard.

He showed us hidden nests, named the birds, helped us feed the hens and pigs then told stories of their dramatic escapes and re-captures. **He taught us to stalk the broody hens** to find their 'lay-away nests'.

Jen, Barbara, Michael, Ernest and Judy with Uncle Edward
(Tears)

He made the farmyard an enchanting playground. He set up swings in the 'chaff house', gave us rides on the tractor, helped us climb trees, built the biggest and best bonfires for us and erected the finest swing across the stream.

He seemed to sleep a lot, probably because of the strenuous physical work and the fresh air. **We tickled him on his bald head with a feather on a string** and woke him up, grumbling about the bloody flies annoying him. His work clothes were shiny with 'muck'. His trousers were always held up with string and his coat was fastened in the same way.

We watched him trim the paraffin lamps, pluck the geese and hens' feathers at Christmas (we never saw him kill them) and chop the piles of logs for the fires. **He shushed us when he showed us the new piglets** or when we went near the sitting hens.

He asked for very little but he was human and had his 'weaknesses'. Grandad enjoyed a pint of bitter, never at home, only very occasionally at the Welfare at Woolley Colliery.

He almost sang to his pipe of baccy, which he especially enjoyed if he could add the stub of a cigar to his mix. Most of all he loved a day at the races and a bet. One year when all the extended family were holidaying in Blackpool together (about 20 of us) **he had a particularly good week at the betting shop** and treated us all, half a crown each to spend at the slot machines and a show on the pier.

Gran Jane was equally hard-working, having six children, six hungry farmhands and a husband to feed every day. Jobs had to be allocated or she couldn't have managed to get through the day. Fetching milk, peeling potatoes, washing up and other general duties were given to her children as they became old enough. They had to be carried out before they left for the **two-mile walk to school.**

As they married and left home and as the farm became more mechanised, fewer farmhands were needed and so **the number of mouths to feed became less**. Life became a little easier for her until

Jane Tear, nee Patten, *back row, right,* around 1900
(Tears)

we, the grand-children, appeared. To be allowed to stay overnight was a treat but came with rules. Only when we were able to attend our own dressing, undressing, washing, teeth-cleaning and hair were we allowed to stay. We learnt at a very young age!

Jane Tear on Top Row with baby Barbara in the early 1930s
(Tears)

Aunty Flo, Uncle Cliff and Jen lived in a converted bus on the farm land. **An invitation to stay with them was beyond our wildest dreams.** We watched foxes play in the moonlight outside our window, close enough to touch. We heard and watched owls in the dead of night. We felt so close to nature that we were nature!

Visits from every family were encouraged, especially for Sunday tea. Rationing was still in force so **each visiting family brought a contribution to the meal** - a tin of fruit, cream, meat or salmon. 40 for tea was not unusual, forcing three sittings around the kitchen table, children last. Cricket and rounders teams were formed and games fiercely played, to win. Everyone joined in.

Like all women bringing up a large family and running a home that they were proud of, Gran had to be organised. She had her days for washing, ironing, cleaning but **what set her apart from the rest was her Mondays.** This day she called 'Cobbler's Monday'.

She mended, darned and repaired clothing and household linen **but her main interest was making leather and fur (rabbit)-backed gloves and mittens.** She knitted complicated garments for friends and family, all given as presents. She was equally generous when giving away her cakes.

Tear cousins in 1950 - *back row, from left*, David Tear, John Tear, Jen White, Judy Speight; *front*, Peter Tear, Heather Tear, Michael White
(Tears)

50 years on, Heather couldn't attend, Colleen Landy and Jane were there
(Tears)

Every Thursday she baked for Britain in a coal-fired oven with no thermostat. She started at six o'clock in the morning and during the exhausting day, produced bread, sweet and savoury tarts, buns and cakes, enough to last a week and give away to every neighbour or visitor who came near.

She invited neighbouring farmers to whist drives in her front room (it was enormous) and we had to be still and silent during the game, but when they were carrying out their 'inquest' at the end of each game, we could be as noisy and boisterous as we wanted. The games were halted as Grandad Joe (who never played) lit the lamps as darkness fell.

No electricity or gas meant we had to make our own entertainment, especially in the dark winter evenings. We played cards and dominoes or housey housey if there were enough of us. **We always played for money, the theory being that you learnt quicker!** We still do! And we still play to win!

But like everyone else, Gran had her 'failings'. **She couldn't cope with Joe having a pint of beer,** mainly because he always burst into the song *To Be a Farmer's Boy* when he had had a couple of pints which she found to be very embarrassing.

She soon stopped him and gave him the sharp end of her tongue.

To say she was a dominant character is an understatement. She was a matriarch. She held the family together, commanding respect and giving love. **A benevolent dictator.**

Jane was born in Leeds and Joe near Doncaster. They married in Pontefract and took a very circuitous route to finally settle in and near Woolley Colliery.

They had six children, each one born in a different village as **Joe travelled from farm to farm searching for work** as a shepherd, a ploughman but mainly as a horseman. They lived in properties owned initially by Fountain and Burnley's and later by the N.C.B.

These were Manor Farm up Fountain Square and Bottom Old Row at Woolley Colliery. They recognised his skills as a horseman which helped him secure Moorhouse Farm at Haigh, which he worked for them with the help of six farmhands. **He grew cereals and fodder for the pit ponies** working at Haigh and Woolley Colliery and cared for them in their retirement.

When he retired from farming, what was left of the family moved to 17 Bluebell Road and Joe spent the rest of his working life as 'horse man', on permanent nights at Woolley Colliery pit.

Jen James, nee White, … and my very special childhood on the farm

I lived in a 'caravan', a converted bus at Moorhouse Farm, where my Gran Jane and Grandad Joe lived. It was heated by a pot-bellied stove in winter and lit by paraffin lamps. In summer doors and windows had to be left open because it got so hot. The horses soon saw an opportunity to take apples from the table. When other kids watched dogs and cats at play, **I watched foxes and rabbits in the field outside my 'bus' window.**

Jen White with Moorhouse Farm in the background in the summer of 1945
(Tears)

Both the farm and the caravan had only cold water on tap. There was a well which was used in emergencies, like the time in 1947 when all the pipes froze. We were trapped by snow which reached well up the farmhouse door. Grandad Joe bridled up Major the shire horse and led him backwards and forwards to the well carrying buckets of water until a path like a tunnel had been made. **We all had to sleep at the farmhouse that night,** all the kids in one bed, with rugs thrown on to keep us warm.

Water was heated in the copper boiler at the side of the fire range. It was filled with cold water, the lid put on and a fire lit beneath it. It was large and reached quite high in the corner of the kitchen and was a great place to play and watch the adults. I dangled feathers on a stick and string to tickle Grandad's head. He blamed the flies!

I remember walking on Woolley Edge, above the farm, with Uncle Ernest and my cousin Judy (another cousin, David, wouldn't have been far behind). We could see the farm below but more amazingly **we could see my mam spread-eagled on the roof of our green bus.** She had gone onto the roof to clean the flues of the pot-bellied stove and got stuck. We had to race down to rescue her.

I spent a lot of time with Grandad Joe. Even though he was extremely busy, every evening, he made the time to find me. **He hoisted me onto the back of Major,** the shire horse used for ploughing, and led me to the stables to settle him down for the night.

Like everyone else, I was given a job. Once, mine was to look after a lamb which had been rejected by its mum. I loved giving it the little titty bottle feeds and cared for it for several weeks. Then, **one day, out of the blue, a 10 shilling note appeared on my breakfast time plate** but no lamb to greet me. At a very early age I learnt that farming was about survival and profit, not sentiment. My lamb had gone to market and I had been given my 'wage'. It was scant comfort.

My distress, (or my skills at rearing animals) had been noticed and my mum produced 13 fluffy chickens, bought in Barnsley Market. They were always sold in baker's dozens.

So the feeding and caring began again but things turned slightly nasty when it became apparent that **they were all cockerels who became more vicious as they grew,** almost pecking out my eyes. Uncles Eddie, Jack and Ernest cruelly taunted them and ran them around the farmyard until they had no meat on them, only tough muscle. We were sick of them by the time they were gone.

Another upsetting memory was a result of my dancing lessons. My mam insisted that I had ballet lessons and took me to Miss Frisby's Dance School in Barnsley. We had to go by train from Haigh station. One day I fell on my way to the station and cut my knee very badly, but my mam made me go in spite of buckets of tears and blood everywhere. Rewards came later. **I appeared at a**

Sheffield theatre as **'Little Miss Prim'** which involved a silver hat box with a pink organza bow.

Joe's tenancy as a farm bailiff was primarily to supply care, food and bedding for the pit ponies at Haigh and Woolley Colliery. A blind eye was turned to anything else he wished to rear. Wartime had brought about rationing so **food was a valuable trading asset.** He bred pigs and had to notify the authorities about the number of piglets born but he always reported one or two less than had actually been born.

He kept these, illegally, for his own use. He fattened them up, had them slaughtered and jointed and finally hung them in the cellars below the farmhouse. My cousin Judy still remembers the sweet smell of them.

I remember the aroma of Gran's homemade bread baking in her fire oven. Thursday was baking day and yes, I had my job to do. **I had to grate and squeeze the lemons,** hugely important if the 'bake' was to be successful. From six o'clock in the morning, oven bottom cakes, bread, cheese and onion pasties, meat and potato pies, lemon curd tarts, Yorkshire curd tarts, macaroons, buns and fruit cake.

Jen White at the seaside with
Michael White, Colleen Landy and
Barbara Landy
(Tears)

The huge kitchen table heaved under the weight of all these goodies. We could choose whatever we wished for dinner but only two pieces were allowed. The rest was wrapped in cloths and put in crocks or tinned or given away to neighbours and visitors. **No-one left empty-handed.**

The outside, double-seated midden provokes memories of a different aroma. I still blame my constipation on having to sit next to Brian Nichols (our neighbours) at the same time. One visitor, who took her handbag with her everywhere she went, visited the earth midden with only a torch for light and accidentally dropped her bag down one of the holes.

We had to sprinkle a pink powder called lye which the midden man left us, down the hole each time we used it. Grandad Joe had to empty it from the back every week when Mr Bannister came with the midden cart. I was kept well away. He refused to use it and **did his 'business' in the field hedge nearby.** Nettles grew well there! Things were even worse when we moved up to the caravan because we had to walk quite a way back to the farm toilets. Potties and buckets were also used, as you can imagine.

My cousin David, a year older that me, lived in the farm cottage along the lane towards Haigh. **Once he tried to drown me in the pig trough.** Then, when out-cropping got nearer to the farm, he tied me to a boundary post on the outcrop and left me. I wasn't found until dusk. Where was my mam? We normally played out from dawn 'til dusk so I hadn't been missed!

David walked to school at Woolley Colliery with me twice every day (we came home for our dinner). It was about a mile and it was through the most beautiful countryside. We walked through fields, over Primrose Hill and finally through Bluebell Wood. **I always got the prize for 'first finds' of wild flowers** such as wood anemones, bluebells, cowslips, violets, campion and ladies' fingers. We had no adult with us on this lonely walk and only once were we scared. We heard that the police were looking for a man who had escaped from an asylum. **We saw him, dressed in his underpants and with a top hat on his head,** as the police chased him through the woods.

It was about this time that **Grandad Joe ploughed up a bomb in the low field.** It must have been dropped during the war (possibly a stray from Sheffield) and didn't explode. All the relevant authorities were informed who dealt with it (I don't remember how) and enjoyed Gran's refreshments before leaving (I remember that!).

Another scare was when I was gored by a young bull. My Aunty Barbara was taking me on the train to the baths. We were walking across the fields near Popplewell's cottages to the station when **a frisky young bullock trapped me in some bushes** and gored me. I have a scar from hip to armpit to explain why I will not enter a field of cows.

But the best scare came from Grandad Joe. Entertainment was either playing cards or dominoes at home (or someone else's house) or going to whist drives and dances at Bretton. Grandad didn't play or dance so he was volunteered to babysit. **He played** *Big Bad Wolf* **with us,** either leading us or chasing us around the darkened house with only a candle in an old-fashioned holder. The house was spacious and the dark rooms became lit as the light from the candle entered. Shadows were long and spooky. They moved as the candle was carried through. **We were scared to death** (but loved it).

Eventually I moved to 3 Bluebell Road, Woolley Colliery, with my mam and dad where my brother Michael was born. On leaving school I began working in Woolley Colliery offices as clerk to the manager. My Aunty Barbara, cousin Colleen and I were lucky to be given the chance to go underground at Thorncliffe's V16's face a week after Derek Ezra had visited in 1975 so it was very clean and tidy. I went down the shaft in the cage but I left my stomach on the surface. **I travelled to the coal face on the paddy** and then crawled on my stomach in a yard-high tunnel to watch the men work the shearer. When they rammed the roof support into place to allow the shearer to do the return strip, I thought the bloody lot was coming down. Great wit, camaraderie and humour kept me going along with gifts of sweets to keep my saliva going.

Jen White's parents Cliff White
and Flo Tear with Laddie the dog
at Moorhouse Farm
(Tears)

The twist of the story is that **it was the slag from the mines that finally buried Moorhouse Farm** but on walks with my dogs I get as near as I can. I think I could pinpoint where it was. The farm has gone but nothing could bury my wonderful memories of a wonderful childhood with a wonderful extended family, mam, dad, grandparents, aunts, uncles and cousins.

Jean Jones, nee Rhodes - Those were the days, my friends…

Each day of the week had a different job allocated to it, not like nowadays when you can wash, iron, Hoover and dust all in one day.

At our house it was:-

      Monday - washing day,
      Tuesday - ironing,
      Wednesday - bedrooms,
      Thursday - windows outside and 'donkey stoning',
      Friday - shopping,
      Saturday - maybe free,

And Sunday was for church, visiting family and friends and **during the war years, it was a 'faith tea'** which meant that if you went to visit someone you never went empty-handed.

And just as each day had a job allocated to it, we knew what day it was by the dinner before us:-

      Monday was cold meat, chips and beans,
      Tuesday was hash with either dumplings or pancakes,
      Wednesday was liver or sausage with chips or potatoes,
      Thursday was meat and potato pie and mushy peas,
      Friday was fish and chips from the fish shop,
      On Saturday Dad made us sliced taties and onions with corned beef on top. And

finally Sunday was a roast beef dinner with a joint big enough for Monday's cold meat and Tuesday's hash.

Just to add a little adventure to our diet, after the war, boxes of food were issued by the pit. It was khaki-coloured, containing **khaki-coloured tins with no labels.** You never knew what you were opening, peaches or pilchards!

I had to make my contribution by earning pocket money at my Great Aunt Annie's house on Bloomhouse Lane. Every Saturday, I cleaned her kitchen and living room by washing the oil-cloth floor. Then I had to wash her outside toilet, steps and windowsill and finally donkey stone them. **My payment was two boiled eggs with soldiers for lunch** and a shilling.

My brother Stuart always liked animals. We had quite a variety - dogs, rabbits and ferrets. One day, our brother Don was feeding the ferrets when one bit his finger and wouldn't let go. He ran up the garden with it hanging on his finger, long before the Richard Whiteley incident.

Jean, Malcolm and Stuart Rhodes, with the Top Row in the background
(Rhodes)

But the most unusual animal was a fox. **We all treated it like a dog and took it for walks on a lead.** Foxy was given to him by Uncle Chuck Rhodes and Punch Douglas, who was a pit baths attendant at Woolley Pit. He lived up Jebb Lane at Haigh and his part-time job was as a gamekeeper. He had found the cubs when he dug out a lair.

Doreen Sykes nee Wraithmell - Gonna wash that man right out of my hair

My goodness me, what a chore washday was. **Tuesday was washday at our house.** My dad would be up at 5.30am to light the set-pot fire to get the water hot. When June, my sister, had gone to work and I had eaten my breakfast and was on my way to school, my mam would start the washing.

She had a wooden mangle, a rubbing board, a posser and two peggy tubs. One tub was full of hot water from the set-pot and the other had cold water. There were only cold water taps in our homes then. She used an old grater, kept especially for this job, to grate a block of Fairy soap into flakes into the hot water tub.

Then the hard work began. First of all, **white clothes were put into the very hot water.** Collars and cuffs of shirts and blouses were rubbed with the block of Fairy soap then rubbed on the rubbing board until clean.

Not satisfied with this, the 'whites' were pushed back into the hot water, then agitated or 'possed' with the posser. Next, they were lifted out and put into the cold clean water tub for a rinse. In those days **nearly everything was 100% cotton or 100% wool.** There were no mixed fibres or nylon.

Clothes were graded according to colours and set around the kitchen in appropriate piles. Next into the peggy tub were the lighter colours, followed by darker and darker ones. The fire under the set-pot had to be kept in and well-stoked because water was constantly taken from it to keep the water hot in the

Doreen Wraithmell in 1953
(Wraithmells)

tub. **The final ones were my dad's pit clothes.** Just imagine the amount of clothes, nappies, towels, sheets and blankets to be lifted about for the large families.

When everything had gone through the tubs, they had to go through the mangle. This was an iron frame supporting two wooden rollers and a great handle to make them go round. The rollers squeezed out the water and so now the clothes were ready to be pegged out to dry. **If it was a wet day, they were dried round the fire on a clothes horse** or hung on a rack which hoisted up to the ceiling to dry overnight.

The day after was ironing day. There were no electric irons. They were called flat irons which were made hot by standing them near the open coal fire. You had to have two because you ironed the clothes that needed very hot irons first then as it cooled you put it back near the fire and picked up the other so you could continue.

So **really, washday lasted two days.** You must remember that my mam had to cook meals for the family coming home from work and school, all at different times, at the same time as she was washing or ironing. A housewife did not have an easy life.

Joyce Parling, nee Brown - Carrying on with the washing day blues

Washday was usually on a Monday, well for every other woman in the village apart from my mam. **She was always a free spirit** and would wash either when she felt like it or when we had no clean clothes.

In the old house on the Low Row, a boiler in the corner of the kitchen was filled with cold water, as we didn't have hot water. Then a fire was lit underneath it. Sometimes if we had no soap powder my mam would grate a bar of green Fairy soap into the water. In went the lightest colours first, and as the water came up to boil the clothes were stirred round with a big stick.

After a good boil they were put into a tub, then through a mangle to squeeze out the suds. These suds were put back into the boiler and the next load put in, sometimes more water had to be added. The washed clothes were then rinsed and put through the mangle again. If it was a fine day they would be pegged out on the clothes line, but only if the wind was in the right direction i.e. blowing towards the pit yard. Otherwise **when you brought them in they were covered in sooty deposits.**

As the copper came to the boil the whole house would be full of steam, which gave us a chance to practice our writing on the steamed-up windows.

Washing in winter was a different matter. If the weather was bad the clothes had to be dried around the house. Clothes horses were filled and put round the fire, and the rest of the room soon became rather cold. Lines were strung against the ceilings and clothes hung up. **Sometimes you got fed up of wet sheets slapping round your face.** But I think it is the smell of wash day that stays in the memory, a clean steamy smell, which with modern appliances, tumble driers and automatic washing machines, you never get.

My mam never did her ironing in one go, she ironed as we needed things, or we just put them straight on from the wash. The irons were flat irons, which were heated on the fire, then rubbed on a cloth to remove any debris. Temperature was tested by spitting on the iron, if it sizzled it was hot enough. Most clothes were made of cotton, linen or wool, so there was no need for thermostats. Cottons were starched, collars, pillowcases, even handkerchiefs. They stayed cleaner longer, but my were they uncomfortable. Net curtains, for those who had them, after being washed were rinsed in either a dolly blue for white nets, or a cream dolly for cream nets. It brightened up the colour, but washed out at the next wash.

After we moved to the council house in Bluebell Road things got much easier for mam as we had hot water, but for a few years washing was still done in the old way. As children on hot days we would strip off and **climb into the tub and tread clothes just for fun.** With the introduction of the electric washing machine the old rubbing board became a musical instrument, they were used by the skiffle groups.

The Browns hanging out at 7 Bluebell Road, *from left,* Michael Brown, Roy Whittles, Jim Brown, Philip Crossley, Anita Crossley, Olive Brown with baby Susan, and Mick Brown *(hiding)*
(Browns)

I was about 10 when we got our first electric washer, what with that and hot water it certainly made washday easier for mam. The tub was still used to rinse in, but the machine had electric rollers, and on bad days we had two rooms and an airing cupboard to dry clothes in, so life became more pleasant. **Mangles became obsolete** with the invention of the twin tub, I think they now fetch ridiculous prices at antique fares and junk shops.

I can't ever remember my dad helping with the washing or ironing, but I can remember when I was very young that he only had one good shirt but lots of collars which were attached with studs, which made one shirt last all week. So I suppose they did their little bit by not making too much washing.

Houses were cleaned by a brush as most people had linoleum on their floors. Your mam got down on her hands and knees with a bucket of suds and a floor cloth and washed the lino. On the lino was a big pegged rug, usually made by your grandma from old coats etc. This was hauled onto the clothes line and beaten to get the dirt out. **Windows were cleaned with water and vinegar** and polished off with newspaper, which left your hands black from the print. In the old house on the Low Row we had a big black lead fireplace and oven. This had to be polished every once in a while to keep it shiny and bright. I think the polish was called Zebrite, which was put on with a brush and then rubbed up until it was shiny, a dirty job though.

The only cleaning products I can remember are **Vim, Wimsol and Fairy soap.** Toilets were cleaned with Vim then Wimsol was poured down to make them smell sweet, Wimsol was bleach. In the old house we had to go across the road to use the toilet, and I can't remember if two families shared one toilet.

Certain jobs were done on certain days. Monday was washday, Tuesday was ironing day, then there was a baking day, **a swilling down of your steps day** to be followed by scouring of the steps, which was rubbing a scouring stone along the edge of each step to leave a thick white or yellow line. What was the purpose of this I don't know to this day, but it was done religiously every week and woe betide anybody who trod on them.

All in all a lot of wasted time and energy on menial tasks that didn't really matter to us but obviously did to our mothers and grandmothers.

My mam was very good at sewing, she **could make us new dresses out of next to nothing.** Often when we were small, me and my sister Olive wore matching dresses. Then as we got older it would be the same material but a different colour.

Apart from the clothes you went to school in **you only had one best dress,** which was kept for Sunday Best. Your school clothes weren't very good, lots of hand-me-downs and jumble sale clothes,

but every Whit Sunday you had a brand new outfit of clothes, in which you paraded round the streets with the Sunday Schools on Whit Monday.

On Whit Sunday when you had your new clothes on, you would go to people's doors to show them, and they would give you coppers. Money was very short at this time, so how your parents managed to produce a whole new set of clothes and shoes was a miracle, although I think **a lot of it was bought on the tick** (as it was called).

My mam was often left with lots of pieces of spare material, as she sewed for other people as well, and when she had enough she made a patchwork quilt, and when we were in our teens, Olive and me, we would point out all the dresses we could remember from being small, **it was almost like a social history of our childhood.**

Lots of things had to be mended because you couldn't always afford new. Socks as they began to wear at the heel were darned, collars on shirts were turned, and sheets when they were wearing thin in the middle were cut down the middle and turned so the thicker outer edges were in the middle.

The tallyman was a regular caller every Friday night (as Friday was pay day at the pit). Most things were bought on the tick,, anything from clothes to furniture, from bicycles to electrical goods. To us as children it was just the way of life.

My dad played in Woolley Prize Band and every Christmas Day the band went all round the village playing. **Every time they stopped they were plied with drink.** I can't remember many Christmas days when Brownie wasn't merry, and as his birthday was Christmas Eve, I think he lost quite a few Christmases.

My dad never had an allotment but Mr Teal and Mr Bogg had one each just below the big house, which was the pit manager's house. Mr Teal seemed to grow a lot of flowers but **Mr Bogg was a vegetable man,** he once gave me the biggest cabbage I had ever seen for my mam. I could hardly carry it, she was very pleased to receive it and made quite a few meals.

When we moved to Bluebell Road the garden at the back was quite large and my dad started growing vegetables, my favourites were the small potatoes called chats, which my dad used to deep fry, then put salt and vinegar on them they were delicious.

I really can't remember very much about meal times as we had our dinners at school and **our teas were a jam sandwich in your hand** whilst playing out. I do remember the Sunday roast and my mam's Yorkshire puddings. I have never tasted any as nice as hers, how on earth she managed to cook them in a coal oven with no thermostat I'll never know.

The Sunday joint had to cover three days, Sunday roasted, Monday sliced cold with fry up, Tuesday hashed up with vegetables. I've tried many times to make hash like my mam did but always failed.

Treats were few and far between, but we did have a few. **Threepence to spend at the shop was like being in wonderland,** there was so much to be had, kayli and Spanish, bubble gum, 2oz of Yorkshire mixtures and many more, I think the equivalent amount today to 3d is under 2p.

Another treat was when the ice cream man came, everybody rushed home to see if they could have one. If you were lucky you joined the queue at the van, **the unlucky ones could be seen usually crying.** Being given 9d to go to the dance on a Friday night was a big treat, as was the Saturday morning matinee at Darton Picture House.

My dad had an aunty, Aunty Dora, who lived in Doncaster. It was always a treat when she came to stay with my Grandma Brown in Darton, because she always brought treats of barley sugar and liquorice sweets. They tasted like heaven.

The fair came to Darton every year. I can remember being taken for the first time the noise and the lights were so exciting, **My mam put me on**

The Browns go to Blackpool, *left to right,* Olive Brown, Molly Tovey (holding Glyn Tovey), Hilda Empsall, Barry Tovey, Anita Crossley and Derek Tovey
(Browns)

the **little roundabout,** with our Mick and Olive. After the first go they wanted another. Whilst it was going round for the second time my mam had to drag me off as apparently I had turned green. That was the last of fairground rides for me, just watching them used to make me sick. As I got older I enjoyed the dodgems, and did have a few rides on the caterpillar. **I think my mind was too occupied with kissing the boys that I forgot to feel sick.**

Some of the best treats didn't cost anything. In summer my mam and Aunty Molly would take us all off to the dyke. **A picnic of jam sandwiches was packed,** with Welfare orange juice to drink, but just by the fact that your mam and your aunty were with you made it such a special time.

Money was always short but **I can't remember feeling deprived,** as we were mainly all in the same boat, some just a little bit worse off than others. If I asked for some sweets and was told no, I would go round the village to see if any women wanted anything from the shop and **would run errands,** which usually ended with 2d or 3d, with which you could by 2oz of Yorkshire mixtures or some kayli and Spanish. Sometimes we didn't have the money on a Monday morning to pay for our school dinners, and I can remember asking Mr.Walton if we could pay for them on Tuesday when my mam collected the family allowance.

We didn't have many holidays as children I suppose because money was short, but **we always went on the Bullet trip** and got our half crown spending money for which you could have eight goes on the funfairs at 3d a go, and a bag of sweets.

The school ran a savings bank where you deposited say a shilling a week into a small bank book. **When you had £1 you were given a big bank book.** I always wanted one but never had one. Pauline Hughes used to put in 10/- every week, which to me then was a fortune.

We didn't need much entertaining as we more often than not made our own. Sometimes some of the older men would start a game of cricket, tip it and run, and they let everybody join in even girls. We played out until bedtime both summer and winter, it was usually bedtime by the time we were called in. **We listened to the radio if it was raining,** *Dick Barton Special Agent, In Town Tonight* even the football results, hoping we had won £75,000.

Life was harsher when we were children. Not only did your parents give you good hidings so did teachers, and the local bobby wasn't averse to a quick clip round the ear. Punishments for wrong-doing were usually being sent to bed or your legs slapped.

Bullying wasn't tolerated. If a bigger boy hit a smaller one, his father would hold him (the bigger boy) and let the little one hit him back, and this seemed to work. There didn't seem to be any serious problems such as drugs. **The worst that happened was mainly swearing** (pit talk) which wasn't allowed, and scrumping apples and pears up the Old Lane. If you were caught doing either a good hiding would follow. If you got into trouble at school then went home and told your parents, you got another good hiding for getting into trouble at school.

You certainly had respect for all adults. You were not allowed to interrupt when an adult was speaking, if two adults were having a conversation and you were seen to be listening you were sent away with the words 'little pigs have big ears' ringing in your lug holes (as they used to be called).

When the local bobby Mr Calvert was on his tour of duty around Woolley Colliery, the moment you saw him **you stood perfectly still until he had passed.** I sometimes wonder as I've got older whether it was respect or fear, perhaps a bit of both. You really were taught respect because another saying I remember was 'don't cheek your elders' and if you did you could expect a clip round the ear.

Dave Bogg - But domestic dreams do come true!

The two Old Rows did not have hot running water and of course no bathrooms. It was a case of the old tin bath in front of the fire. In all of these houses they had a set-pot which was a very large cast iron basin that had a fire underneath it

All the hot water for the house was heated in this and you had to ladle the hot water out of this

Annie Bogg on the front step
(Boggs)

some of the things we would have on our sandwiches for tea.

I remember once going to the home of a guy I knew from school called Norman Lambert and his mother gave me sandwiches that had chocolate spread on them. **I thought they were rich.** In the early 1950s our household used five loaves of bread a day. I called at Gallons on Darton every day for them.

In the 1940s rationing was indeed pretty harsh. You had got to name a shop that you went to get your groceries. **We got to always calling them the rations** and even after rationing finished it was hard to get out of the habit. The old Co-op at Darton always gave you sugar, rice, flour, etc,. in blue bags and cut the butter with a wire very much like the cheese. **Dried eggs were another delicacy** that we had to endure.

Today we take for granted that central heating has always been around. When we were young, once winter came the **upstairs never saw any heat** and we had

and into the bath and then of course send it out in the opposite way. Wash days would see this filled and kept going all day and then when the wash was done **all the kids would be put into the set-pot for a bath.**

For the women of the house it was a very hard life, as house-cleaning and the washing were extremely hard jobs. Tuesday was washday in our house on the Old Row. The set-pot would be filled with water and a fire lit underneath it. This was needed to fill the peggy tub so the wash could commence. **My mother started her wash at 6am** and it would be 6pm before she had finished. The reason for the long day was simple; it was uneconomic to just wash a few things through as the equipment required to do the job was too time-consuming.

Food was always a problem. **For most of us the staple diet was bread and potatoes** as they were most plentiful. I have had a love affair with the humble spud for all of my life, that's why I weigh almost 17 stone.

The traditional way to have Yorkshire pudding is before the main meal with gravy. This had nothing to do with it being a delicacy but more to fill you up so that you didn't want as much dinner.

You never went without your dinner as it would be the next day before it came round again. Bread and jam, dripping, condensed milk, sugar, treacle were

Annie Bogg, Dave's mum, in 2002
(Boggs)

The entertainers - Jim Pendlebury is on the stretcher and Arthur Grayson has the clipboard, but the identity of the lady is unknown
(Pendleburys)

frost on the insides of the windows as well as the outside. We used whatever was available to keep warm and in the 1940s rationing made sure that no-one had much of anything. Everything was utilised, including any overcoats that were available.

The steel plate out of the oven would be warmed up and wrapped in cloth to make the beds warmer. A house brick would also suffice for the same purpose. I suppose today it sounds rather crude to have to resort to these methods. But where-ever there is a will people will always find a way. **These were times that were so different from today.** It is always going to be difficult for someone who never had to do these things to imagine just what it was like.

Friday night in our household was always music night as then **my mother deloused us all.** I don't know what they called the stuff she used but even today if I got a smell of it I would know what it was.

It made your head itch more than the nits did and I'm sure it took a layer of skin off in the bargain. If we got a cold we would always be rubbed with either Seven rubbing oils or camphorated oil. Both stunk to high heaven and everyone knew what you had on.

Whitsuntide is a name today that is largely forgotten as now it is called Spring Bank. However in the 1940s and early 1950s it was very important as then it was the time that we all got new clothes. Our parents would have been saving the clothing coupons for a year to get us kitted out and a finer set of kids could not be seen anywhere than we were. **The churches and Sunday schools had Whit walks** to show off all the kids' new clothes. But underneath it all, it was hard for families. The only good thing I can say is that everyone was in the same boat.

Jim Pendlebury (real name Edward) was an artist in his own right. He dressed as Al Jolson with a black face and all and was very good. Right up to his death him and his wife Connie would go on holiday and **Jim would entertain the guests in the hotels** he visited. Jim had a younger brother called Eric who managed to get the nickname of Dash. When he was young he would fly around at high speed but **one day went headlong into an open door** and the name stuck.

At school in the 1940s we used to sing the songs of Stephen Foster from the Deep South of America such as *Swannee River, Old Black Joe* and *My Old Kentucky Home*. I even got these to sing at Darton school. These songs were of places that living at Woolley Colliery I could never dream of ever visiting and **I could have been on the moon the distance seemed that great.**

However in 1998 my wife and I did a car trip from Canada all the

Jim Pendlebury as Al Jolson
(Boggs)

way through to Florida in the South and we crossed the Swannee River. This had a major impact on me as this was one sight that I never expected to ever see in my lifetime. I don't think there has ever been a more fulfilling thing for me.

David Mason - The heart of it

Every Friday I was taken to visit my grandparents, Bob and Hannah Mason, who lived on the old Top Row. **The black-leaded fireplace, with oven and hearth, was the heart of the small room.** I sat and played with pieces of string kept in an old brass kettle in front of the roaring fire. My Grandad's pipe rack hung just out of reach on the wall. I was two years old. The front room was dark, heavily-curtained and rarely used.

Football star - Derek Tovey
(Toveys)

Derek Tovey - Woolley Wanderers against the world!

...now we were in upper juniors we had the field to ourselves (small kids didn't argue with Don Rhodes, Malc Rushton, Aggy Travis, Phil Margy *et al*) **Our footballing skills were honed to perfection.**

We must have impressed Greenwood because he entered us into a football competition at Ossett. He even managed to get us a football strip. **It was a black and tan quartered shirt with black shorts and black and tan striped socks.** It looked fantastic.

The only person in the village not pleased with it must have been Paddy McNamara who lived near the Hudsons on the Bottom Row on Woolley Colliery Road. He was Irish and black and tan had a very different meaning for him.

Then we tried it on. It must have come originally from some South Pacific island rugby team. **It buried us completely.** Greenwood told us not to fuss and roll over the tops of the shorts and roll up the bottom of the shirts, as well as doing the same with the sleeves. I looked as though I was wearing a bustle, but we had to manage.

In a good wind the spare material under the arms and crotch could have billowed and sent us air-borne. Geoff Booth, however, went one better; he had a pair of football boots to match. They had real cork studs with three nails in each stud that went through the soles and straight into his feet. It's a good job that they did, otherwise when he turned round the boots would have remained in the original direction. **He could stop every ball that came his way** but

Derek Tovey, *front row, right*, with his football mates
(Browns)

Derek Tovey as a baby, with Molly Tovey, Olive Brown, May Crossley, June Blackburn, Kathleen 'Aunt Grete' Blackburn and Barry Tovey
(Browns)

somebody else had to clear it for him because he couldn't lift his feet off the ground.

In goal was Eddie Joyce. He later became a policeman and was often found on duty at Barnsley football matches. He wasn't in the mounted section because he would have had to carry the horse around. Just the sight of him was enough to stop any bother. He was big even then.

Our star players were Malc Rushton and Don Rhodes. Glen (Haggis) Travis, Johnny Winkler (face of a cherub - round and smiling - built like a dumper truck) and a few others who could run non-stop for hours on end and were worth their weight in gold. I was good in short bursts. **In fact I was really good until I got the ball,** then my feet let me down badly.

Let me explain this. Normally, at school, I would play in pumps or wellies. I could get my feet under the ball and get it to go where I wanted it to go. I could also get some distance on it. **For the competition dad got me some new boots,** well at least they were new to me. I think they'd belonged to ar Bas. He was older and much bigger than I was and had camel feet. They also had four studs in each sole which caused me to rock and roll about on a surface which was hard. **The toe caps were solid and about two inches high** which meant that I couldn't get my feet under the ball to lift it.

This wasn't much good for this competition as I was on the wing. This was where my problems began - not a question of skill, you understand. At the competition we had another problem, it was also a proper leather football. It took us all some time to get accustomed to it.

On the big day I can't remember a team talk. Our strategy was simple: **if the ball goes somewhere, everybody follow it** (except the goalkeeper). The first time I tried to kick the ball I thought I'd kicked a bollard. It looked like a soggy Christmas pudding and as the day wore on it got heavier. The second time I touched it I tried to head it and it knocked me to the floor as if I'd been kicked in the face by a pit pony.

Later that day, after the match, I found the marks the laces had made on my forehead. During the whole of the afternoon I didn't manage to get in one decent cross to head in. It's probably a good job because I don't think anyone fancied heading that ball anyway. They could have been carrying the scars to this day.

I found that **the best way to kick it was to swing my leg like a golf club** and toe-end it. This way at least I got some distance. We managed to get to the final until our tactics were sussed out. We met Crofton in the final. Our tactics didn't work from the outset.

Wherever we chased they'd loft the ball to another player where we weren't and when we chased it there he'd pass it to another place where we weren't. Poor old big Eddie. **It was like a coconut shy.** He tried valiantly but couldn't keep them all out. I was so knackered that I kept out on the left wing (and was congratulated for my positional play afterwards).

I can't remember the score but I remember that we were sporting about it and chanted, "Crofton won the final, boo, boo, boo, boo. Crofton won the final boo, boo, boo". **Some of the dads joined in** once they'd got the hang of the refrain but an embarrassed Greenwood got us quickly out of the way and on the bus.

Collect your thoughts

My first memory is of my brother Joe carrying me over his shoulders up the hill to school, screaming, swearing and kicking my wellies off every five yards. I was four. It didn't take long to settle in when I realised you could run in the woods at playtime.

Even so young, we spent hours in the summer holidays bird-nesting in Woolley, Nottton woods, Monkey wood and Bretton Lakes. Punch Douglas was the gamekeeper there and if he caught us, he would smack us across the legs with his stick, then pat us down so heavily that **any eggs we had in our pockets were scrambled!** My younger brother Don was our climber. He could be at the top of a tree like a monkey reporting the contents of the nest and collecting eggs. I had to look at the floor. I daren't watch him. We all had collections then, even in school. My brother Roy and Jackie Waller were in charge of it.

At conker time, **I remember collecting conkers on the road to Bretton** and throwing sticks and stones into the tree to knock them down. Don threw half a house brick from one side of a tree and it hit Roy's head on the other side of the tree. Stitches required!

Phil Margison

Remembrance.

I have some friends, some cherished friends,
Whose names are treasured dearly,
So to those friends, my dearest friends,
This card is sent sincerely,
To tender you, heart greetings true,
And not good wishes merely,
But with the prayer that you may share,
All things you love most dearly.

A Christmas card sent to the Tear family in 1942
(Tears)

Chapter Four
Mams 'n' dads

Strict or soft, batting or badly, where would Woolley kids have been without them?

Terry Taylor reminds us what mams and dads were for...
Whatever was going on in the village **all our parents seemed to be involved,** and I think the most important of all was that our parents were in total charge of the household. Nobody argued too strongly with their parents, **we were taught respect,** probably the hard way, but it worked.

And Dave Bogg makes us think...
The one glaring fact that I remember from being young is that **I can't remember anyone ever getting a divorce.** Most families stayed together. I guess it's too easy to get a divorce these days.

...before he remembers his mam and dad, Annie and George
My mother was born at 30 Union Street Barnsley on June 15, 1916. My father was born at Sculcoats, Hull on July 9, 1904 and died on this same day in 1976 aged 72.

I was born at 6 Woolley Colliery on of February 12 1939 (Sunday) and lived at this address until I was 10. In July 1949 we moved to a brand new house, 16 Bluebell Road.

My mother died on October 25, 2005. Her maiden name was Annie Jordan. In the 66 years that I knew her **I never once heard her swear** and I do believe that must be quite remarkable. I asked her several times why she never swore and she simply said, " I didn't think it would make any difference, so decided not to as there was no advantage in it".

She was 23 when I was born and had been married five years. My father was 12 years older than my mother so was 35. I will always remember my mother with great affection as she looked after us with great ability and the care that she gave us was of the best.

I can sum her up simply by these words - she was **Simply Outstanding.** If I have to come back in some future years and have the choice to pick who would be my mother it would still be her.

Poor but smiling - Annie Jordan (who became Dave Bogg's mother) holding Arthur Howard, with Clifford Beecroft and friends in 1932 - check out the patch on that jumper!
(Boggs)

When she was in her twenties she was quite a stout woman and weighed in at around 13 stone. She always wore a pinny, the type where the top went over the head and fastened at the waist at the back. As there were seven of us in our family **the dinners that she cooked were indeed something** to see. She would make a meat and potato pie using an enamelled sink bowl and place a cup in the middle of it to support the pastry it was so big. The meat usually was corned beef. Even after all these years it is still one of my favourite dinners and also of my two youngest daughters, who I think like it as much as I do.

This was one of those dinners that did not cost much as potatoes and flour were reasonably cheap and easy to get hold of. My mother used to go through one cwt of potatoes a week and of course we used **five loaves of bread a day.**

She lived in the bungalow almost straight in front of the Windhill centre for 17 years. For the past 12 years my wife and I made her dinner and I would take it on to her. I always looked upon it as payment for what she so unselfishly gave us. At least I knew then that she at least would have one meal a day, as if she had to make her own she would have simply not bothered. I guess for the most of us we have the same feeling for our mothers. Life goes on whether we are here to witness it or not? **I miss many things in my life but nothing more than not being able to see my mother.** R.I.P.

My father came to Woolley Colliery after my grandfather got work at the pit. My grandfather had walked from Beverley to try to find work, this was in 1913. He also managed to get them a house, number 10 on the Old Row where he lived until his death in 1954.

He suffered a stroke in 1972 which took his speech. However this did finally come back but his biggest loss was that **he had forgotten how to play the accordion.** As I was the only one in our family who could play the accordion my father gave me it. I still have it today, although I very rarely play it. I could also play the mouth organ by the time I was eight. My father suffered another stroke in 1974. This disorientated him so much so that my mother was just unable to cope with him. He spent his final days in Kendray hospital and died on his 72nd birthday, July 9, 1976. I guess one could say **he had a hell of a hard life,** working 52 years in the pits.

Billy Crossley remembers his mam and dad, Polly and Ernest
My dad was born in Garden Street, just below Dillington dog track, Worsbrough Common on December 9, 1913. He was educated at Keir Street School and Holgate Grammar School, Barnsley.

He had connections with Halifax where there are numerous Crossleys. His mother was an Emmet (also common in Halifax) with Irish parentage. A family 'story' is that she was **a blood relative of the famous Irish patriot and orator Robert Emmet.**

Dad met my mam and married her on the island of Malta and in 1937 mam came to live at Woolley Colliery. **Coming from Malta,** this must have been a tremendous change in her life. I'm glad and proud of her for doing this.

I was born two years after my dad was involved in the biggest single disaster of the Second World War. He was being evacuated when **his troopship *Lancastria* was dive-bombed** just off the Port of St. Nazaire in the Bay of Biscay in France.

'The evacuation of British troops from France in 1940 did not end with Dunkirk. British forces were still being rescued two weeks later when Britain's worst maritime disaster of World War II took place.

Churchill immediately hid the news from the public. In 1940, after Dunkirk, to reveal the truth would have been too damaging for civilian morale.'

BBC News - Maritime Disasters of WWII:The Secret Disaster
LANCASTRIA (June 17, 1940)
The Cunard/White Star passenger liner Lancastria, the former Tyrrhenia (16,243 tons), is bombed and sunk off St. Nazaire, France. While lying at anchor in the Charpentier Roads on the estuary of the River Loire, five enemy planes dive-bombed the ship which sank in 20 minutes taking the lives

George with Annie Bogg at the wedding
(Boggs)

Nathan Jordan, Annie Jordan's dad and Dave Bogg's grandad
(Boggs)

Dave Bogg's aunt Elen Jordan in 1912
(Boggs)

Dave Bogg's grandparents Nathan Jordan, Annie Elizabeth Hayes Jordan, with their daughter Elen, aged two in 1894
(Boggs)

George Bogg at his son Alan's wedding in 1963
(Boggs)

Buggered Bogg - George Bogg asleep on the beach at Scarborough 1957. Son Dave had taken them in his first car
(Boggs)

Nathan Jordan - the elder and the younger
(Boggs)

of around 2,000 troops and over 1,000 civilians. The Lancastria had been converted into a troopship and set sail from Liverpool on June 14 to assist in the evacuation of British troops and refugees from France.

Survivors estimated that five thousand lives were lost. **Dad was rescued** and nursed back to health for six months. I certainly would not have been here had he died.

He returned to the pit where he became heavily involved in Union duties. He later became a Wakefield District Councillor. With us, **he was a hard taskmaster** and we were always wary of his reaction to any of our wrong-doings. It did us no harm in life's conformity.

He had **nationwide fame** for a while in 1949 on the radio. He sang *The Angelus* in harmony with uncle Bill and Frank Crossley and Tommy Waller on Kennth Horne's *Spot the Winner*. Almost everyone who had a radio locally listened to them sing. We were so proud that evening and still are.

Mam didn't know when she was born but thought it was on April 30, 1912, in Floriana, Valletta, Malta. It wasn't until she checked with Somerset House that she discovered that it was actually May 5. So, like the Queen, **she had two birthdays each year** after that. Her mother (maiden name Zammit) owned her own bus company. She met and married my grandad Bray, a merchant seaman from Curry Rivel, Somerset. I never knew him.

My mam was the **epitome of motherhood.** She loved and cared for us but could be harsh enough to let us know where we stood. A slap from her was sufficiently hard to say she was boss. She was loved by most of the village and by my cousins too. However, she had the **odd physical disagreement** with old Lizzy Addy, our neighbour.

She wasn't a brilliant cook but **her rabbit casserole was the best in the village.** She went 'spud bashing' (potato-picking) to make ends meet.

We got hand-me-downs to wear from neighbours but Whitsuntide was 'best dressed time' when we all had new clothes. She wasn't dress proud and she always put us first in her life.

She couldn't abide being 'Lady' Crossley, the councillor's wife which appeared on the many function slips my father had to attend in his role as councillor. She was my Mam and we all loved her to her dying day, as with dad too. **They both worked hard to bring us up proper** like all the parents in our little village. Thank you.

Jean Jones, nee Rhodes remembers her mam and dad, Margaret and Wilf

My mum, Margaret, always had some knitting on the go to fill her 'spare' time. She was a very good knitter and we always had hand-knitted jumpers, cardigans, scarves, gloves and hats for winter. **She spent some time 'on the rug' with dad too.** They always pegged a new rug for Christmas.

She helped other cricketers' wives make **teas for both teams at Darton Cricket Club** on the Long Fields when they played at home. I had to look after my younger brothers. My dad and brothers (as they got old enough) had a reputation of being good cricketers.

Dad loved watching Wakefield Trinity play rugby. On one special occasion, the 1968 Rugby League Final, he took his sons in his Commer Cob van to Wembley, London. When Don Fox kicked for a conversion near the end of the game to win and MISSED, he was so upset that **he never spoke to anyone all the way home** from London to Yorkshire.

Dad worked as a winding engineman at the pit. He also made his contribution in the home. He didn't have an allotment but **he grew vegetables in our garden.** He also grew tomatoes and cucumbers in a greenhouse. Nothing tastes as good as a tomato straight from the plant. We had some ducklings because duck eggs made super egg custards but one had a funny wing so **dad had to kill it.** We called him a murderer and wouldn't speak to him for days.

Dad always pickled onions and red cabbage for Christmas. They were stored in jars on the stone

slab in the pantry. One day, (it must have been a Wednesday because mam was cleaning the bedrooms) she came downstairs to find our Malcolm eating the pickled onions which he said Stuart had given him. **Mam found Stuart in the pantry** with both hands in the pickle jar.

She put a mousetrap on top of the jar and told him that if he touched it again it would bite him. Sure enough, she hadn't got half way up the stairs when there was a scream and Stuart was running around with a trap on his hand. In today's P.C. environment, we would have been taken into care.

When we were young, policemen patrolled on foot or on a bike. If he found you doing anything you shouldn't be doing, **Bobby Stathers would give you a clip around the ear** and you had to tell your parents. He always checked. And as a bonus, mam or dad would give you another clip to help you remember. It didn't take long to learn important lessons. **Mam was the disciplinarian** but was happiest when surrounded by her family.

Doreen Sykes, nee Wraithmell, remembers her mam and dad, Clara and Joseph

My dad was Joseph Backhouse Wraithmell. He was born at 48 Top Row, Woolley Colliery. He worked down the pit with his father as a blacksmith's striker and later on the pit top in the screens.

My mam was Clara Tyas. When they married they moved to 54 Top Row to live with my great grandad. **My dad always helped around the house.** He was a very good handyman, painting and wallpapering, but his hobby was his garden and his greenhouse. He also kept hens and geese, as many as 48 hens at a time.

Marion Brackin, nee Coatesworth, remembers her mam and dad, Elizabeth and Lawrence

When we moved to Woolley Colliery dad set to and made gardens back and front to grow vegetables for us. This involved **us all going down to the stables for horse manure;** tons of it! Then up the wood for leaf mould. Tons of that too!

We roped our mates in to help. Soon the garden took shape, **we grew potatoes, broad beans, dwarf beans, and runner beans** all up the front wall. Peas, carrots, beetroot, lettuce and radish. We had rose bushes and azaleas. One year, dad and Uncle Walter Yeadon (he was manager at Co-op nurseries) grafted a black rose. **It flourished that year, 1960, the year Dad died.** But it died the following year. Perhaps we did not nurture it enough.

My dad had a big 28-inch bike, his pride and joy. It was difficult for me to ride having shorter legs, so I put my leg under the cross-bar and managed it that way.

When the cricket season was on we used to go with my dad to the matches. **He was an umpire** at Woolley Village and surrounding areas. I still think the lovely teas the ladies put on were better than the cricket.

I got home from school one day and dad said, "Go look what's in the room". In the corner by the fireside was a coop with two dozen day-old chicks, keeping warm under a Tilly lamp. **Dad built a hen house** down the banking; it looked like Noah's Ark. It was on stilts to deter the foxes, with six foot high wire netting all around.

When the chickens were old enough, they were put in the hut. We used to boil a big black pan of vegetable peelings mixed with meal to feed them, also corn and grit. Then dad acquired a cockerel, **we called him Colin!** What a character he was! He was Joe Louis and Sugar Ray Robinson rolled into one! We were all scared stiff of him.

Dad used to put an old tea cosy on his head as the cock used to fly onto his shoulders and peck away! We all had to feed the chickens in turn and dreaded the job as Colin was such a terror! One year dad decided to sell some cockerels for Christmas, so we fattened them up and Dad killed them.

Beach baby - Jean Rhodes with her dad Wilf at Blackpool
(Rhodes)

Mr Wraithmell with Doreen as a baby, outside
the shared toilet
(Wraithmells)

Lads or ladies?
– Mrs Senior, Mrs Rhodes, Mrs Taylor, Mr Turner and Mrs Booth in Germany
(Rhodes)

A caring community - *top row, from left*, Mrs Warmsley, Eva Senior, Carol Margison, Yvonne Bogg, Sandra
Bogg, Edna Booth; *bottom row, from left*,
Dorothy (second name unknown), Mrs Rhodes, Mrs Joyner, Phyllis Crowther, Unknown
(Boggs)

Doreen Wraithmell, *front*, on holiday with her mam, dad and her sister June
(Wraithmells)

Woolley Colliery - *Ar it woh*

But it fell to my Mam and I to pluck and clean them! What a rotten job! We were covered in red mites from the feathers, but we managed to deliver the birds in time for Christmas.

My dad **suffered with chronic chest problems most of his life,** caused by pit dust and it finally took his life. May God bless you dad.

As well as looking after seven children my **mam cleaned houses in Woolley Village,** three times a week she used to walk there and back. But when the end of September to October came, she went to Rowbottom's farm potato-picking for six weeks. Mrs Crossley and Mrs Weatherall also went and they would walk up to the crossroads at the top of Sackup Lane, where they were picked up on the tractor and trailer and taken to Woolley Village to work. This was a very hard job with all the heavy lifting, but **money was scarce.**

My mam was a very good baker, her teacakes and oven bottom cakes were delicious. She excelled at parkin, ginger cake and feather cake and her Quaker oat biscuits disappeared before they had chance to cool! She also **made lovely treacle toffee.**

One year near Whitsuntide, she sewed six dresses all by hand, putting smocking on the smaller ones. **She sat up through two nights** to complete them for Whitsuntide. My, we all looked grand in our new sandals and peep-toe shoes. Not forgetting our Lewis in his new shirt and shorts.

Mam sometimes went to Darton pictures with Mrs Crossley, Mrs Sanger and Mrs Garforth. **If it was a musical or an Esther Williams film,** she took me. We used to call for three penn'orth of chips from Chippy Harts and my, they were tasty! After dad died in 1960 mam only had 30 shillings pension, so she went to work at Beanlands Mill. She stayed there until it closed down, in 1976. After we had all married and left home, Mam and Lew flitted back up through the wood to Windhill. She sadly died July 2, 2003. May God bless you mam. We didn't have much money but **we had a happy family life.** Thank you.

Pat King, nee Coatesworth, remembers her mam and dad, Elizabeth and Lawrence

As the nights got darker mam started off another rug. She brayed the hessian onto her frame and set to. Our rugs were allus a mainly red multi-colour, with a four-inch black edging, about two and a half yards by one yard. We were all trusted to brod and were proud of our little stints. It never seemed like a chore, sitting by the fire brodding away, listening to the wireless. **Mam spent hours cutting up old woollen coats into strips** and then filling the mixed-up colours into carrier bags.

Black was a problem as folks hung onto their funeral outfits, so mam had to resort to going onto Barnsley Market and actually buying a bag full of black clippings to finish the borders.

I always admired Garforths' brodded rugs, as they often did circles and diamonds in the centre of theirs, while ours were quite plain.

Me and our Mave got into trouble for lending out the rug frame while mam was out shopping. It was never returned, the folk flitted taking our frame with them! Mam never let us forget her fury, and **even into her eighties she would snap,** "Aye, and I could be here brodding a rug if you two buggers ent gyn mi frame away".

Usually a new rug was put down by the hearth on Christmas Eve. After Boxing Day it went up into the bedroom, the bedroom rug came down to the hearth and so moved around, the oldest rugs being in the kitchen.

I remember me and our Sheila being the first to roll on the new hearth rug. **I can still remember the smell of the woollen cloth,** the crispness of the new pile - heaven.

Most people will say they were poor - will brag about it - but I'm telling you, **we were poor and we had nowt,** and that is a fact. All we had was our good name and our pride. We were truly the 'poor relations', all the rest of dad's family had money, but only Auntie Emily on dad's side was good to us. She sent us all Everild's old clothes and toys, so we got some sort of Christmas. **Mam did what she could,** colouring books, crayons, oddments. Aunt Alice, Grandma Wiles' sister, was

good to us too. Whilst we lived at Brick Row she lived next door, and was kindness itself.

Dad was a badly man, he had chronic bronchitis and pneumoconiosis, he coughed and peffed constantly, couldn't walk far without a rest, yet he smoked cigs like a chimney. He was 18 years older than mam, so was an old man to us, especially with his bad chest. Despite his ill health he kept a garden full of vegetables, to eke out the rations. We also kept hens, so **plenty of eggs for mam to do lots of baking** for us, tarts, currant pasty, mince pies and a big feather cake for us to go at, whenever.

Cut and curled for the occasion - Pat Coatesworth
(Coatesworths)

Dad's family were all keen cricketers. Dad also went umpiring round and about Darton and Mapplewell. We went, us kids, sometimes, and **I learnt all the rules of cricket early on.** Dad was a keen reader and Mrs Rhodes changed his books in the mobile library, then I picked them up after school.

We never got smacked. We got threatened often enough, if we cheeked, then ran through the passage, he would chuck the pot hole shovel or brush, it would hit the hollow door, there were several dents to prove it! If we didn't settle down at night he would bray on the stairs steps with his belt, saying we'd get it next! We never did.

Mother's day was never done. The work always exceeded the hours in the day. For years she had nothing electrical to help, no washer or Hoover, no cooker, no fridge. How she ever managed to cook and bake so well I'll never know.

On dull days the fire wouldn't draw, so **mam's temper would fray -** "damned oven - I could sit in it", she would witter (we giggled imagining it), but let the wind rise and the fire would roar away and the oven would burn owt that was put in it - 'burnt offerings' which we still ate. I remember the oven itself blazing up, and mam grabbing a shovel of earth from the garden to extinguish it, of course the chimney would be on fire too, the air would be black with soot and blue with mam's curses. The cats would skiddaddle till it all calmed down. Then the water would bang and thump as the water boiled non-stop, we were always sure it would burst,but it never did.

Dad's health was so bad he couldn't work, and eventually got the sack in the late 1950s, so **we lost our coal allowance.** Our Lewis wasn't old enough to claim coal allowance as a lodger, so we were snookered. Occasionally, we would get the coal in for someone and they'd give us a few buckets. (Coal was delivered by the ton several times a year to all miners, it was dropped at the

Lew Coatesworth with Buddy the dog
(Coatesworths)

**On Brick Row Betty Chalkley shows her dad
Bob Chalkley** *(sitting, left)* **and Walt Margison
that she means business**
(Boggs)

Elizabeth Coatesworth as a young woman
(Coatesworths)

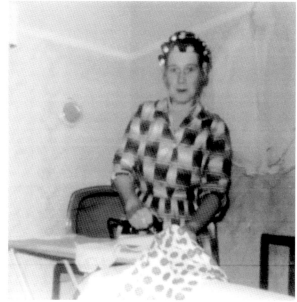

Elizabeth Coatesworth gets on with the job
(Coatesworths)

Edie Chalkley (Betty's mother), *left,* **and
Mrs Hepworth on Brick Row**
(Boggs)

Woolley Colliery - *Ar it woh*

bottom of the drive and had to be manhandled a bucket at a time into the coal house). Only Mr Wilson, lower down the street, sympathised with our plight, as he also suffered with his chest like dad did. He would give us a quarter of his load, his **kindness was a godsend.**

We went up the wood logging, but the wood burned so swift you needed a coal base to make any difference. So, no money, no coal, no warmth, no oven to cook or bake, no hot water for washing and bathing. There was nowt else for it, we had to go down to the wagons and pinch some.

This was a terrifying and shameful thing to do, but what else could we do? We were cold! The wagons were there, and we only picked the coal dropped below the wagons to put into our little noggin bags. Us younger end couldn't carry much, so had to go back several times, facing the bright arc lights of the pit and the rows of buses fetching the night shift to the Colliery.

Dad would crouch under the wagon wheels, **coughing and peffing as he shovelled the coil.** His cig would glow bright as he took another drag, and filled another bag. You could see and hear the drivers and conductors grouped together chatting, waiting for the afternoon shift to come tramping on the Low Row from the pit, to fill their buses. I was always convinced we would be caught, sure they could see us. We even had to pass the night watchman's hen hut, below his house.

Sometimes our mates helped us, as **we couldn't laik art till the coiling had been done.**

After all that a pitiful little pile of coal would be heaped in the wash house, to be used sparingly, with the logs that we had dragged down home from the wood.

We survived it all somehow and things looked up when our Lew got lodger's coal later on.

Mavis Tomalic, nee Coatesworth, remembers her mam and dad, Elizabeth and Lawrence

Dad always kept hens and a cockerel. **He'd get us up early to collect the eggs,** but first he played 'eeny meeny miny mo' on our fists. The 'winner' got to go down the banking withdad to the hen hut, which was on stilts and much higher than us. We would only be six to 10 years old. We went to the hen run which had very high chicken wire all way round, dad unlocked the hut then stood out of the way so that we could open the door. The cockerel was first out of the hut and always chased us round the pen. Dad collected the eggs, then let the hen run. **We didn't escape until he threw their food in.** I never remember actually collecting any eggs.

Mam couldn't always afford a joint for Sunday dinner so Dad would kill one of the hens. He'd tie it up by the legs, hanging it upside down on a hook, high up on the washhouse. Trouble was it used to twitch for a couple of days. He told us watch it until it stopped twitching, which we did (like idiots). He would then pluck it and clean it ready for the oven. It always tasted nice along with the fresh vegetables from our own garden.

Dad always grew vegetables in both the front and back gardens. He did the heavy work and **we were sent to collect horse muck and cowpats.** He told us to poke our fingers in the cowpats and, if they were soft, to leave them for another day. When we had collected some we brought them back and dad mixed them with water in an old peggy tub. **As a treat we all got to stir it round to mix it in** (wow, we thought this was brilliant at the time).

This made his manure to put on the garden before he planted his vegetables.

Dad had an old bike called 'grid iron' and when he was going anywhere he always 'chose' one of us to go with him. I'll give him his due though; he always went slowly on the level and downhill so that we could keep up with him, and guess what? We got to push it uphill for him. We thought we were honoured, I suppose we each in turn thought we were special.

We'd try one foot on a pedal to have a ride and usually ended up with it on top of us. Dad would rescue us though and the fall was soon forgotten. It was massive that bike and it weighed a ton. You have to remember we were only eight, nine or 10 years old.

Jen James, nee White, remembers her mam and dad, Flo and Cliff

My mam and dad lived in a converted green single decker bus just behind the cow-sheds at Moorhouse Farm, just a few hundred yards from the main farm house. My Gran Jane and Grandad Joe lived there. **My dad had bought the bus with his de-mob money** on his return from duties in Africa.

I was four when I first saw him. My mam and I had lived in the farmhouse until then so it's difficult to separate my parents from grandparents in my earliest memories. My mam helped around the farmhouse after I was born and during the time my dad was in the army. It must have been difficult for my mam when my dad came home. She didn't go to meet him with everyone else; **she hid in the broom cupboard instead.**

Derek Tovey remembers his dad, David

Sometimes me dad would join us at weekends playing cricket in the field just beyond our garden fence. When he left Welsh Wales aged 16 **he'd been trained as an electrician** in Rugby and had worked on Stirlings and all sorts of other aircraft during the war. He spent most of his waking hours at the pit as an electrician.

Sometimes we wouldn't see him for days on end, especially during 'bull week' when he'd put in double shifts. This happened just before the annual pit closure during Barnsley Feast Week. The extra money he earned sponsored our trips to Mablethorpe or Brid. Or Rhyl.

He loved his weekends though. **He fancied himself as a bit of a spin bowler** and used to send these slow balls up to the wicket that you were certain you could bash all over the place. Just as you swung at the old tennis ball it would stop, dance around you and hit the wicket.

Because he was there **I'd show off outrageously,** trying to impress him. I soon cottoned on that I couldn't do it with my batting or bowling, so it had to be fielding. I'd dive and run all over the place.

On this one occasion I was keeping wicket and dad was bowling to ar Bas (I think). We'd come out straight after breakfast. **The day was ours.** Bas had started to get the measure of dad's tricks and could read what the ball was going to do, even though he had to squint into the strong sun.

This meant that dad was also trying especially hard. Ar Bas was three years older than me and at least three stones heavier. He also had a powerful arm, so if dad got it wrong and Bas hit it, it meant that somebody had a long chase to fetch it.

The game became more intense as they both vied for an advantage. **One tricky ball came straight through Bas's guard** and kicked off over my right shoulder. I knew dad would be disappointed that I'd missed it so I turned immediately and saw it nestling in the grass. I hoped nobody else could see it, as they were all forward of the wicket.

I made as if it was still moving and dived on top of it. As I got up I made to throw it but **my right arm wouldn't work.** I looked at it and there was a peculiar U-bend in it, near the wrist. It was only after I'd thrown it back under-arm with my left that the pain came. I held my arm and skriked like a baby.

Dad told me not to be so soft. Now THAT really did hurt. I could no longer keep wicket so somebody else went behind in my place. What made it worse was that Bas was caught behind a few balls later. He stumped off mumbling and threw the bat down and dad made me pick it up.

It was my turn to bat. Dad was obviously pleased, flushed with his success. He made me take my guard and **in his largesse he sent up one of his 'donkey drops',** a high looping ball that invited you to smack it.

I could only use my left hand so merely poked the bat forward as though Freddie Trueman had sent down a stonker. Everybody groaned and told me what a useless person I was (when dad was there nobody was allowed to use any bad language).

Ladies' day - a trip to London for, from left, Kitty Routledge, Mrs England, Mrs Hunter, Minnie Dixon, Minnie Chadwick, Mrs Hudson, Mrs Pendlebury, Beattie Burbridge, Mrs Birkinshaw, Gertie Sanger and Polly Crossley
(Boggs)

Outside 19 Old Row are two Joe Burbridges, father and son, who stands with his wife-to-be, Beattie
(Boggs)

Mr and Mrs Pendlebury outside their house
(Pendleburys)

Mrs Pendlebury in her turban, and a friend
(Pendleburys)

And Mrs Pendlebury and her son John, just before he joined the Mounties (joke)
(Pendleburys)

He bowled a couple more and the atmosphere of excitement declined rapidly. Everybody was dischuffed that I'd managed to spoil the game. **Dad came up to me, in a huff,** and had a look. He told me that there was nothing wrong with it but mam should have a look, just in case, so we upped stumps and walked the short way down the field to our house.

Mam had been a nurse in a previous life, before motherhood and the WAAFs. The fact that she'd worked in a psychiatric unit at Storthes Hall cut no ice. She was a nurse. She had the authority. She was also good at dressing wounds of all shapes and sizes on kids of all shapes and sizes and had developed good diagnostic skills.

"It's brokken," she announced.

"Can't be," said dad.

"'e needs tekkin' to 'ospital." The pronouncement was final.

"Who's goin' to tekk 'im?"

"You brokk it, you tekk 'im." And that was that.

We finished up on a bus to Beckett's Hospital in Barnsley. Now this did scare me. There had been many tales of people, perfectly healthy people, walking in, never to be seen again, or coming out with something that they hadn't bargained for.

I came back with a huge white pot up my arm. I could just about wiggle my fingers and only just bend my arm at my elbow. Whoever did it must have had a sense of humour because they set it with my thumb sticking out at right angles so anything with long sleeves was impossible to wear.

"At least you might be able to thumb us a lift back." This was dad, who though still dischuffed, could see that I must have been in pain.

Joyce Parling, nee Brown, remembers her mam and dad, Olive and Jim

My dad always worked shifts in the pit, days, afters and nights. Days started at about 6am until about 2pm, afters would be 2pm until 10pm, and nights 10pm until 6am.

I never bothered much which shift my dad was on until I became a teenager and got interested in boys. My **dad always said I had to be in before he went on nights,** which I was. Then when he had gone to work my mam would let me go out for another half an hour.

My mam also worked when I was small, she used to clean the pit offices, and I can remember getting showered in Mr Rimmer, the pit manager's office with Pauline Hughes when we were about eight. After she finished work my **mam and the other cleaners would go up to the top canteen for a cup of tea.** Whilst I was waiting for her outside I used to run up and down the steps.

At the side of the steps was a rockery with plants that looked like miniature fir trees. In this little wood, as I called it, lived a little elf, who could only be seen by me, and as I ran up and down he ran up and down in the little wood. We were best friends for a long time, and I can't remember exactly when I outgrew him, but I still remember him with fondness, even if he was a figment of my imagination. When I was in hospital with scarlet fever **I had a little white rabbit living in my cot, that only I could see.** I must have been a sad child.

We were always invited to our cousin Margaret Empsall's birthday parties. She was an only child so always had parties and as we never had any, we all looked forward to going. When I was about six, our Mick, seven, and our Olive eight, we were getting ready in our Sunday best clothes to go to the party, but our Mick's hair wouldn't lie flat. As my mam had nothing to flatten it with, **she put some beef dripping on it.** Our Mick was really upset and refused to go to the party because he said he smelt like the Sunday dinner.

And she remembers forgetting who her mam and dad were...

When I was four years old there was a scarlet fever epidemic at Woolley Colliery. I had it, my brother Mick had it and Pauline Hughes had it so bad it left her with a bad heart.

A sheet soaked in San Izal was draped over your house door. The children who were ill were taken to Carrgate Isolation Hospital near Wakefield. Your stay in hospital could be anything from four to six weeks, and **in all that time your parents weren't allowed to visit you.** I remember them once coming and looking through the window. You couldn't take anything such as toys or books in with you. If you did they had to stay behind because scarlet fever was very infectious.

My time in hospital was spent in a cot and I wasn't allowed out of it for the full six weeks. I'd just about forgotten how to walk when I was better. When my mam and dad came to collect me I remember being in the arms of a nurse and clinging onto her crying because **I'd forgotten them and didn't want to go home with them.** I wanted to stay at the hospital.

How times have changed and I think for the better.

Joyce Brown's Grandma and Grandad Crossley - the little girl standing is Connie Crossley, who died in 1940 aged about 28, and the baby is Ernest Crossley, the father of Bill who wrote the poem on page four
(J.O Pauling)

Good friends, good times - Mr and Mrs Tovey and Mr and Mrs Brown at 27 Bluebell Road
(Browns)

Jim Brown with his beloved newspaper - the *Daily Herald* - in Bluebell Road
(Browns)

Home from the war - Jim and Olive Brown in 1940
(Browns)

Jim Brown in his army uniform - he was in the Honourable Artillery Company, Hac, Hacs for short, firing the big guns which shot down German Bombers over London
(Browns)

Olive Brown shows the boys how it's done
(Browns)

Smart chaps - Jim Brown, *centre*, with Dick Scurr and friend at a wedding
(Browns)

Jim Brown in his younger days - note the scarf, fashionable again!
(Browns)

Chapter Five
Teenage years
Do you remember the first time?

A teenager before they were invented

My dad was very strict and didn't allow us to roam the streets. We had to be in by a said time, but we went to the pictures in Darton, the film was changed every two days, with a special film being shown on Sundays. We went to the pictures with a jam jar and 2d, the jam jar got us in, 1d was spent on sweets and other 1d on a bag of chips from Chippy Hart's on the way home.

There were seven picture houses in Barnsley, and several places where we used to go dancing including the Drill Hall, Cuban, Georges and the Baths. We also went to the Youth Club. At the end of the Top Old Row was the fire station, we went there for beetle drives, whist drives and bingo.

Flo Howard, nee Hayward, born 1932

What about 'big school'?

When I passed the 11-plus to go to Thornes House the uniform had to be bought from Southcotts in Wakefield, so off we went, mother, Stuart and I. The school crest was on the blazer badge, a stork with one foot on a shell. Mother had on her best telephone voice as we were mixing with mothers and pupils from Wakefield Girls' High and Q.E.G.S.

On seeing me try on a blazer Stuart said in a loud voice, "Dunt ger ah Jean that wun, t' bird's gorra brocken fooit".

Jean Jones, nee Rhodes

When I passed my scholarship the High School had a strict uniform, including liberty bodices, and I know my mam struggled to put mine together. When we changed from gymslips to pinafore skirts she went to Wakefield to look at the new style, drew a copy of it,, bought some material and made mine. We also had to wear beige ankle socks, mine were white dyed in tea. I never felt any different from the rest.

As we got into the fourth and fifth years we found the rules a bit tying - you weren't allowed out at lunch time, it was frowned on for girls to be seen going around Wakefield, no associating with the boys from Q.E.G.S., always have your full uniform on. Occasionally we did break the rules but luckily we were not found out. I realise now that all those rules and regulations that we kicked back at really did set us up for later in life and stood us in good stead.

Those years allowed us to form friendships with girls from very different backgrounds to what we had. Our dads were mainly miners, theirs were doctors, lawyers and dentists. I left school at 16. The thought never entered my head to go on to university.

Joyce Parling, nee Brown

What DID we do for fun?

For most people the Colliery was a place to go to, not through. Coming out of the wood from Brick Row to the top of Bluebell Road was like rediscovering a 'lost civilisation'.

It seemed to me like a community that wasn't used to strangers because I did feel there was some interest in me but no hostility or suspicion.

The lads followed me through the village, ragging me about the dog (a white Alsatian) and pretending to be terrified of it. I grew up in a neighbouring pit village but Woolley Colliery was unique, a close-knit community where everyone knew everyone.

Best of all there were lots of young people of my age and they all seemed to be clued in, 'street wise' as they say today and they had lots of freedom to boot.

Carol Brown, nee Shaw

No one had a television, I think Mrs Tear, Jen White's nan, was the first to get one, and some of the kids used to go to her house to watch *Robin Hood*. She charged 3d which she gave to the church. I used to walk up through the wood to my Aunt Alice and Uncle Walter's house to watch their television, they lived at Brick Row. My dad used to go across the road to Jumps' house to watch the cricket.

Pat King, nee Coatesworth

My proper teenage years started when I joined Darton Youth Club. The leader was Mr Roberts. Youth club nights were Monday and either Wednesday or Thursday. We mainly went to bop the night away, but we also had a bit of culture, with meetings, and a PE class, for which we wore tiny full flared skirts. After the P.E. class finished we bopped in our little skirts. I was elected Youth Club secretary and had to take down the minutes at meetings and then write them up for the next meeting.

Mr Roberts arranged for a group of German teenagers to do an exchange visit. They came from Dortmund in Germany, which was very industrialised. They didn't feel too much out of place as the pit was still up and running. They came during the school holidays and stayed with different families - we had a girl, Heike Stegmann. She made a beautiful apple pie, and showed my mum how to make it the German way.

Joyce Brown, nee Parling

Friday nights, a gang of us would congregate on the 'stute steps, under one of the windows. We took it in turns to stand on the ledge to peek in and see all the lovely dancing. We were either too young or had no money, or nowt to wear, there were many reasons why we couldn't 'go to the ball'. However we enjoyed hearing Mr Turner announcing 'The Palais Glide' or the 'Gay Gordons'. It was wonderful, we felt part of it.

Mavis Tomalic, nee Coatesworth

In winter me and Kath used to sit on the form in the fish shop to keep warm. Phyllis gave us a few chips and some fish bits to get rid of us. When we went out of the fish shop we just wolfed them down, they tasted delicious.

Pat King, nee Coatesworth

Mmm. Chips...We all seemed to go tatie-picking didn't we?

We went tatie-picking at Norris Horsfield's Pear Tree Farm, down Woolley Village. He would take us back to the farm for our sandwiches. Whilst there we would do a bit of apple and pear scrumping. Nozzie would tell us to get them from over the wall as they were much sweeter, it was only later that we found out the apples and pears over the wall belonged to the Smiths' farm.

It would be dark when our Marion, Mave, Pat, myself, Mary Bogg, Kath Armitage, Gordon Garforth and some others set off in a morning and dark when we arrived home at night. Nozzie would sometimes let us take some taties home, depending what mood he was in, he would also give us a lift on the horse and cart to the top of Woolley Edge. We always had a good laugh even though we weren't paid much, I think it was seven shillings a day, 35p in today's money.

Pat King, nee Coatesworth

Birds of a feather -
Violet Buckley, and her friend,
thought to be Dorothy Child, outside
a pigeon hut
(Buckleys)

Jean Rhodes' brother
Stuart Rhodes with his
furry friend
(Rhodes)

Brian James keeps a close eye on Jen White and
Marion Coatesworth strutting their stuff in Blackpool
(Coatesworths)

Potato picking at Rowbotham's farm in Woolley Village, including, *middle row, right*, Elizabeth Coatesworth and Polly Crossley
(Coatesworths)

The Butlins' Likely Lads - *from front left*, Unknown, Lew Coatesworth,
Alan Bogg, Malcolm Sanger and Trevor Garforth
(Coatesworths)

I loved going to the pictures…

I remember going to Darton Picture Place to see the coronation. Me and Cath Armitage went every Saturday to the matinee. I had to earn my money by running errands. I used to post a letter every Friday for Mrs Bellin - she gave me sixpence and a bag of brandy snaps. A gang of us went to see *Singing the Blues* with Tommy Steele. Coming home we were all singing it at the top our voices.

One day I had been laiking out at the Row end when I saw me Mam and our Joan getting onto the seven o'clock bus. I knew where they were going and I was desperate to go with them! They were going to see Elvis in *Jailhouse Rock*. As the bus set off, summat came over me and I jumped on the platform and shot upstairs to join them.

Mother nearly had a fit. She played 'holy hell'. Said I had to get off at Darton as she hadn't enough money to pay for me as well. I defied her, wouldn't get off at the Bullet, so she set about tidying me up. I was scruffy, in a raggy old tweed swagger coat with buttons missing. Mam took her hanky and spitted on it then cleaned my face, rubbing vigorously and cursing me all the while! She combed the lugs out of my hair none too gently, by which time we'd reached Barnsley. We sat right at the front in the cheapest seats, craning our necks up at the screen. But it was wonderful, I saw Elvis for the first time and I was in heaven! Of course I never heard the end of it but I wasn't bothered, I had seen Elvis!

Pat King, nee Coatesworth

I went to the pictures to see all the musicals, at that time the shows were continuous, and I sat through them twice, sometimes longer. I would memorise all the songs, and sing them to all my friends at the Row end, telling them the story.

Olive Whittles, nee Brown

There was never much to do on a Saturday especially if you didn't have a boyfriend, if you had one the back row of Darton pictures was where you would normally be found. Every Saturday night my mam made a big dish of stew and after the pictures or wherever we'd been we would turn up for a dish of stew.

I was going out with a boy from Kexborough at this particular time and we called for our supper at mam's. Always there was a bottle of brown sauce on the table to go with the stew, as my boyfriend put the sauce on his stew my mam said to him, "lick the bottle if you want to, our Joyce does". He finished with me shortly after., I wonder why?

Joyce Parling, nee Brown

Rock Around the Clock with Bill Haley was on at the Odeon. Jen, Joyce and myself went to see it. We were wearing our stiletto heels and had our flat clutch bags, trying to look all grown up. When the film started everyone was stamping their feet. Some got up in the aisles to bop but were thrown out of the pictures.

Marion Brackin, nee Coatesworth

Remember that night we ended up in Blackpool?

The all-night dances at the Towncroft started at midnight and went on until 4am, and were an important part of proving we were 'growing up'. I was 14 years old and all my mates were going to the dance but my dad said I was too young. I put him under constant pressure until he finally said that if I could beat him at 'Chinese Whist' (a card game with some cards covered and some showing and the person winning most tricks won the game). I won. And to be fair, he kept his word and allowed me to go.

On one occasion, we made a bit of a holiday out of it. With Joyce Brown, Margaret Empsall and

Pat Chadwick (I think) I started the evening at Darton flicks then went onto the dance. We had a smashing time.

As we walked home at dawn, we spotted the stationary train on Darton station and on an impulse, jumped into the guard's van (the last carriage) as it was pulling out and bopped all the way to Blackpool. We had almost no money between us.

We were enjoying ourselves so much that we lost track of time and had to run all the way from the Pleasure Beach to the Central Station to catch the train home (guard's van again). We only just made it. We had been 'missing' 24 hours and I can't remember getting into trouble for it. Nowadays there would be total panic!

Jen James, nee White

Oh, I'll never forget that night!

When I was 16 a crowd of us went to the pictures on the Sunday night at Darton Picture House, the on to the all-night dance at the Towncroft, when that finished we walked to Darton and caught the train to Blackpool. It was the Cooper trip to Blackpool which went every year at Easter or Whit, on a Monday and left at 5.30 am.

We had a smashing day in Blackpool, not getting back until after midnight. I can remember feeling like I had been up forever. I never did that again, but often went to the all-night dances. The feeling walking over the fields to Woolley Colliery at 4.30 in the morning is something I'll never forget - the whole world seemed clean and bright and quiet despite the pit.

Joyce Parling, nee Brown

We all loved dancing though didn't we?

Someone opened up a little building with a juke box in it down Monkey Park, you could bop the night away. The place used to get packed, but boy did we have fun. Not everybody could bop to really fast songs, and one in particular was very fast, *Freight Train*, and the floor used to clear and I would get up with this one boy, I can't even remember his name, we would bop away, and when the song finished he returned to his friends and I returned to mine and we never conversed at all. I don't think I ever knew his name. It was the time of ,"Are you dancing? Are you asking? I'm asking. I'm dancing".

Joyce Parling, nee Brown

We used to go to Bretton Village Hall dancing. We would walk to Darton Church and catch the Huddersfield bus to Bretton. There were quite a few young farmers who had access to transport, usually one of us managed to click, so we could have a lift home.

One Christmas we had a shared present of a Dansette record player. I remember teaching my brother Stuart to dance to *Hoots mon, there's a moose loose aboot this hoose* by Lord Rockingham's Eleven - eat your hearts out Kaiser Chiefs and Arctic Monkeys!

Jean Jones, nee Rhodes

At the age of 12 or 13 I started going to the dances at the 'stute and made the journey from Staincross down the Ram Jam and Bloomhouse Lane, in the dark, on foot, much to my mother's anxiety. The walk was only disturbed by the occasional startled pit pony behind the hedges, which would galvanise roosting blackbirds into action, scaring me to death.

I would emerge from the darkness of the lane past the Welfare to the welcome sight of the orange lights which lit the road to the village. The only orange street lights I'd ever seen, they seemed very glamorous back then.

Leaders of the pack - Marion Coatesworth and Pete Brackin get ready to roll
(Coatesworths)

Olive Brown, *left*, putting on the style in Blackpool in 1953
(Browns)

Mike and the Meteors play Woolley Welfare in the late 1950s - *from left*, Brian Swallow, Terry Taylor,
Mick Wilson and Jack Joyner and on the drums, Geoff Whyke
(Taylors)

Pat Coatesworth in 1963 with Bluebell Road in the
background
(Coatesworths)

Rebel without a cause - Dave Bogg revs it up a gear
(Boggs

It was the highlight of my week. I even managed to get my mum to buy me a sachet of Sunsilk shampoo especially for the occasion, a real luxury. We learnt how to do all the old time dances and everyone loved it, but I think that everything started to change when *The Tennessee Wigwalk* arrived, closely followed by Bill Haley and *Rock around the Clock*.

Mick, my hubby-to-be, would peer in through the windows with the rest of the Colliery lads, laughing at us all. They wouldn't have been seen dead prancing around with a lot of girls. Their flat caps, lumber jackets and hobnail boots said it all!

Carol Brown, nee Shaw

And we loved Blackpool!

The whole of the Youth Club took these German exchange visitors on an outing to Blackpool. It was a very hot day and we all got sunburnt. On the way home everybody paired off (as you do). I ended up sitting with Bob Hudson, he came from Woolley Colliery, and we canoodled all the way home.

I met up with him at an event last year and asked him if he remembered the trip home from Blackpool, but he said no. When I saw him again later he finally admitted that he did remember. I remember it fondly as part of my teenage years. I hope he does too.

Joyce Parling, nee Brown

My first holiday without my parents was to Blackpool, with three work friends. Mornings were spent on the beach with lots of people (teenagers) from the Youth Club - it was a lovely friendly time.

Nights were spent dancing at the Tower or Winter Gardens ballroom. We danced to wonderful bands, Jack Parnell and Ted Heath. This was where I met a lad from Middlesbrough called Danny Mahoney. We spent every night dancing, and it was sad when we had to part at the end of the week. We kept in touch for a few months, and then like all holiday romances it fizzled out. I really enjoyed that holiday, but at the same time I was homesick for mam and dad and my brother and sister.

Olive Whittles, nee Brown

The things we wore!!

I can remember Kath Armitage and myself wearing shocking pink and lime green socks. They were the latest craze, we thought we were very daring, but we were stopped from wearing them at school.

Round about the same time we both had our hair up in a ponytail, if that's what you could call it. We had about thirty clips holding our hair up, and the only bit of ponytail to be seen was a wisp of hair about two inches long. We thought we looked like film stars.

Pat King, nee Coatesworth

I had those socks too...

I once wore a shocking pink pair to the High School under my beige regulation ones. I was on tenterhooks all day in case they were spotted, as uniform was very strictly adhered to. If I had been found out I would probably have been suspended.

Joyce Parling, nee Brown

And I really did like nice clothes!

My teenage years seemed to start literally overnight, one day I was out on roller skates, flying up and down the village, aged 14, next day I had my first pair of high-heeled shoes, with matching clutch bag and gloves, in fashionable tan.

By the mid-1950s, a new craze had taken over called rock and roll. We all dressed as Teddy girls, drainpipe trousers, so tight our mothers put zips in them so we could get our feet into them, baggy jumpers, or we had full flared skirts, with a tiny waspy belt, back-to-front cardigans and layers of sugar-coated mesh petticoats. I don't think our parents knew what had hit them.

As I was still at school at 16, I didn't have a large wardrobe. I used to sneak out in our Olive's when she wasn't looking, but her friends started to tell her if they saw me. She was none too pleased, but she'd got some of them from Aunty May, who at that time was about 28 and very glamorous. Olive had first choice as she was the eldest.

Joyce Parling, nee Brown

And hair...

One of the fashions was to bleach your fringe (like Zoe Newton, the milk advert girl) I did mine and loved it. Unfortunately Miss Knott did not, and I had to change it back before school the next day. One girl in our year tried to lighten her hair with bleach, she had a sore forehead for weeks.

Joyce Parling, nee Brown

Lads though - what were they like?

Like all isolated communities, the Colliery was well served by enterprising 'businesses'; the tallyman who sold everything from clothes to hardware, the pop man, the cig machine man, the ice cream man and the visiting greengrocer. I bought my first new bike and Teddy suit on the tick, from a tallyman from Royston. Later there was Ian Moody doing the rounds with his catalogue.

Dunford's sold fruit and veg from a lorry which proved to be too much of a temptation for us lads when it was left unattended. Visits from the police to the 'usual suspects' were not unusual. These visits were not about vandalism or malicious damage to person or property, just roguish, laddish escapades. A clip round the ear 'ole from police or parent usually solved it.

Mick Brown

In his teens our Stuart got himself a tattoo kit. From then on, on Sunday mornings the kitchen was taken over by a gang of youths waiting for their turn for a 'work of art'.

Ginner Hunter had Popeye on his upper arm, which wasn't to his liking, so it was covered over by a swooping eagle, unfortunately it had Popeye's legs hanging from its undercarriage. Mum spent her Sundays striding over lads, trying to get Sunday dinner ready, in between dabbing Dettol on the tattoos.

Jean Jones, nee Rhodes

Different youth clubs used to be invited for visits and one night the Royston lads turned up. They certainly brightened up the place - they were all Teddy boys with D.A. hair styles, pale blue suits, winkle-pickers or blue suede shoes and thin ties. We thought all our birthdays had come at once, they were even good looking. The one I picked out was Big H (Harold Hemming) he was called Big H because there was another Royston lad called Harold Madeley, smallest of the two, so he was Little H.

Joyce Parling, nee Brown

Hanging out - Jim Brown, *far right,* and gang
(Browns)

Team spirit from the 1940s - Trevor Buckley is *top row, far left,* and the goalkeeper, Joe Turner, played for Barnsley
(Buckleys)

Dave Bogg digging for coil at Scarborough
(Boggs)

Olive Brown with Theresa Parks in Blackpool
(Browns)

Baby Susan Brown with Anita Crossley and Olive Brown outside 7 Bluebell Road in the early 1960s
(Browns)

Madonna eat your heart out - Margaret Empsall and Joyce Brown aged 15
(Empsalls)

Mick Brown joined the Navy at 17 and served on HMS Raleigh and submarines
(Browns)

In 1957 I was 18. This was the year that I bought my first car, a 1935 Ford Eight. It was already four years older than I was then. It had the registration number of BOK 200. I only had this car for about six weeks when I swapped it for a 1935 Austin Twelve. It was handy at that time as I had a cousin who had a scrap yard in Lundwood and he let me swap them.

These early old cars taught me how to repair them. I have never been stuck with anything that needs fixing and have always worked on the principle that there is no such word as 'can't'.

Dave Bogg

Remember that Christmas when you nearly burnt the house down?
My cousin Jen (White) and Marion Coatesworth and I were allowed, for the first time, to be alone at number 3 Bluebell Road whilst the grown-ups spent time at my Gran's house at 17 Bluebell Road, enjoying a Christmas get-together.

The very ancient, artificial Christmas tree stood on the sideboard decorated with old, painted, burnt-out torch bulbs and bits of silver toffee paper (wrapped around God knows what), dangled from the threadbare branches. It was post-war and money didn't stretch to anything better, but this tree did have something a bit special.

Candles were stuck into little holders and attached by clips - one at the end of each scrawny branch. I persuaded Marion to light them.

The tree was so dry and old that it went up in smoke in a split second. It crackled.

I was in complete shock and stood rooted to the ground.

Thank goodness Marion had more presence of mind. She grabbed the tree by the wooden base and rushed through the house to the back kitchen door and threw it into the snow in the back garden where it sizzled. I think Jen ran up to number 17 to get help. I was still rigid with fear. When all the fuss had died down and no-one really blamed me (it really was my fault) Aunty Flo thanked me because the insurance money paid for a new sideboard, carpet and redecorating. I suddenly became a hero!

Judy Speight, nee Tear

Do you think we had more freedom then?
Although we had quite a lot of freedom, like being allowed to go to the late dances, our parents were quite strict about the time we should be in. If I wasn't on the 10 o'clock bus home after the Youth Club, my dad used to be out looking for me, he chased me home more than once. When he was on night shift we had to be in before he went to work, but after he'd gone my mam used to let us go out for another hour.

Joyce Parling, nee Brown

And we did all work from an early age...
My first job was as a posting clerk for Cantors, my wage was the princely sum of £2.1s .6d per week. I remember spending my first week's pay on a Rhona Roy blue pleated skirt. I didn't half get into trouble for that. Every week you had to tip up to your mum and she gave you back your spending money. Mine was £1.00, but out of that I had to buy make-up, stockings and pay my fares to work. It didn't go very far, so it was good to have a boyfriend who was working, he would pay for you into the pictures.

I worked in Barnsley and started at nine o'clock, but as the bus ran every hour on the hour and arrived in Barnsley at about 8.20 am, this was far too early so I started to go by train. I had to walk over the fields to Darton. I was used to that as I had spent five years walking over the fields to get the 'school specia'l. Jen White worked in Barnsley so we used to make the journey together, often having to run like mad to catch the train.

Joyce Parling, nee Brown

When I left school, my mum and dad enrolled me at Leeds Comptometer School. I know that they had to scrimp and save to afford it. I went with Margaret Empsall (now Ellis).

I caught the six o'clock bus out of Woolley Colliery bus station to Darton where Margaret joined me. Together, we caught a bus to Bretton then changed to one bound for Wakefield. Finally, we took a bus to Leeds, arriving just before nine. A three hour journey, to be repeated on the way home.

On the first day, we arrived at the college at two minutes past nine. The 'she devil' who took the class wasn't pleased and split us up, me to the front of the class and Margaret to the back. We hated it and after two days, we couldn't face going back. However, we kept up the pretence of attending the three week course but instead of going to the college, we spent up to lunch time in coffee shops then went to the lunch time 'Bop' at the Majestic Dance Hall with Jimmy Savile as the D.J. Oh Happy Days!!!!!

Then we were sussed and another chapter closed.

Jen James, nee White

We all got married in the end...
I met my future husband at the Youth Club in 1956. I was 17 and he was 18. It was a few months before we became serious. With his friends and mine we went dancing to the Embassy Ballroom, and to 'free and easys' at Clayton West club.

Then friends waned off and Roy and I were married at the church in Woolley Village on September 26,1959. It will be our Golden Wedding soon and we've been very happy.

Looking back I enjoyed my teenage years.

Olive Whittles, nee Brown

"I loved her from the moment I saw her..." - Sandra Bogg, nee Berry, at sweet 17
(Boggs)

My wife would give me merry hell if she knew that I had told you this....we were married in March 1962. What you have to remember is my wife then was only just 19. The general form for a night out was to go on a pub crawl in Barnsley as there were a lot of live rock and roll groups that played in the pubs.

We had only been married for about six weeks and we were in a pub called the Wine Shades. Today it is Barclays Bank. We had got seats even though the pub was quite full when suddenly she went blood red and shot up in the air and said, "we will have to go!".

I thought someone had felt her up and was ready to take on the whole pub. Anyway we got out into Queen Street and I said to her, "what the devil's up with you?!" , only to be told we had to go home again. She then told me the reason was she had just realised she did not have any knickers on. It must have been making her feel that she knew something was not just right.

I thought it was hilarious. I had visions of all the young men diving on the wet floor in an attempt to see up her dress. But I guess for a very young lady it was grossly embarrassing. Needless to say we had to go home...

Dave Bogg

Three brides for three brothers - Alan, Harold and Roy Bogg married Mary, Elsie and Linda Smith from Bridge Street, Darton in 1967. It is still thought to be a record
(Boggs)

Pat Coatesworth and Ian King receiving a lucky horseshoe from niece Lynn Brackin
(Coatesworths)

Man-to-man - Dave Bogg with brother Alan at his wedding to Sandra, at St Thomas's Church, Worsbrough Dale, December 1963
(Boggs)

Good luck charm - Jen White and Brian James with Colleen Landy in 1959, at Woolley Church
(Tears)

Doreen Wraithmell, *centre,* at a wedding in 1959 with Cath James
(Wraithmells)

Chapter Six
The pit

In the beginning was the pit, but that was just the start of Woolley Colliery

The story of Woolley Colliery begins with George Fountain (1806-71), who was living in High Hoyland in 1851 as a coalminer and a farmer of 20 acres. By 1861 he had moved to Moorhouse, Haigh, but now as a colliery proprietor as well as a farmer. His ownership included Haigh and Darton mines.

By 1871, Fountain had handed over the farm, which had grown to 180 acres and the colliery, employing 93 men and 53 boys, to his son Joseph (1832- 1904).

By 1881 and 1891??? he had a farm of 550 acres and lived in Haigh Hall (Jebb Lane) and his daughter Annie Christine had been born (1874).

The following 30 years would see a World War, a General Strike and a Depression when coal production would have fluctuated along with the availability of a workforce. As mine owners, the wealth of the Fountains would have depended on their employees.

Whether the provision of houses was to attract and maintain workers or whether they had a social conscience and wished to improve the miners' lot is debatable. Whatever the reason, houses appeared in Fountain Square, Darton and Woolley Colliery in the late 19th and early 20th centuries.

On the death of her father and brother, Christine became a wealthy woman, but she was shortly to move further up the social ladder when she married Sir William Sutherland,a favourite of Prime Minister David Lloyd George. The couple lived in Birthwaite Hall.

Sir William Sutherland, a Liberal Party politician and Private Secretary to Lloyd George, married Annie Christine Fountain, now 47 years old, in 1921. She partly owned George Fountain and Company Ltd which was taken over by the National Coal Board in 1947. Sir William took over the running of the mines.

…from our house, we watched carriage after carriage arrive at the church gates carrying gentry in their best. We saw Lloyd George. We'd never seen anything like it before or since!

Joe Senior *(see p69)*, **Church View (Rose and Crown car park) remembers August 1921**

The Woolley Coal Co. Ltd was formed in 1867 and handed over to Fountain and Burnley in 1896. This company had extensive local mine holdings.

…Lady Sutherland breakfasted in bed with a view from her window of the winding gear. If the wheels stopped, she sent a servant to find out why. It meant men were not going down and coal was not coming up!

Local hearsay

Sir William and Lady Sutherland died childless within two months of each other in 1949 and their estate was auctioned.

A collier boy (and man) was he

I started work at Woolley Colliery in 1942 and worked underground for 46 years until my retirement in 1978.

I was a 'ripper', ripping the coal from its seam and paid by how much progress we made along it. It was measured in yards and I often represented our team in talks with the management to decide on the rate of pay per yard. Later years were spent as a deputy when I wielded the yard stick (which I still have).

I have many memories of the pithead and yard, the baths, the long walk from and to Higham, the dark, the dust and the day one of my workmates lost his life and the days when I was seriously injured.

I remember the freedom of my allotment, playing and watching cricket at Woolley Welfare and dancing in the 1950s at the working men's clubs, Barnsley Baths and the Three Cranes.

Sometimes, on a Friday afternoon, I took my son back to the pit yard to collect my wage. I taught him to shout my check number through the window. He thought it a great game when a little brown packet containing cash magically appeared.

It's history now.

Tommy Howarth, check no. 3597, aged 90

Top job?

When I left school I did 16 weeks of underground training. The pit and the mills were the main sources of employment for youngsters leaving school but my dad was adamant that I was not going down the pit.

I took a job on the pit top doing whatever needed doing, from working in the screens to pony driving. I eventually went to be a blacksmith's striker, working for my wife's Great Uncle Clarrie, who, according to his own son, was a brilliant blacksmith, but a hard taskmaster.

My Uncle Frank told me about the fossil of what looked like a giant snake or reptile that was found embedded in the coal face but it was smashed to smithereens in the blasting.

Mick Brown

Don't stick fast lad

When I was 16 I worked in the Thorncliffe seam at Woolley Colliery on the 16 Darton level which used to take us then an hour and twenty minutes to get there.

Needless to say it was also red-hot out there. My mother, God bless her soul, was very good at keeping my pit clothes clean, that is if I took them home. For the most part I have to say I just did not do this, so my socks would stand up for themselves and I had just to walk into them.

In the pit canteen they sold a product called Wondermend. This was a liquid in a tube and was used to stick a patch on a torn pair of trousers. One particular day I stuck a patch on my trousers to repair same. I did it in rather a hurry but it worked very well.

I only found that I had a problem when I came to take my shirt off and discovered that I had also stuck the patch to my shirt which made it impossible to take it off. The only way I could take it off was by tearing the shirt. The other guys in the same locker bays were rolling about laughing with tears running down their faces at my antics to extricate myself from the shirt. And they sure didn't let me forget it.

Dave Bogg

A cool dude - it's Harry Bird, a coal-leader for Fountain and Burnley
(Tears)

Living in t' pit yard - the pit and the Old Row, 1910. Notice the school, top of the photograph
(United Villages)

Birthwaite Hall - the home of Christine and Sir William Sutherland
(Old Barnsley)

Faceworker's payslip, thought to be from the 1940s
(Unknown)

The wedding of Miss Annie Christine Fountain to Sir George Sutherland at Darton Church in 1921
(Courtesy of Barnsley Libraries Archives and Local Studies)

A hard day's night and no pithead baths
(Unknown)

Going underground in 1975 - Jen White, Roy Firth and Colleen Landy prepare to visit the face
(Tears)

Home coals to roost
(Taylors)

Woolley Colliery - *Ar it woh*

One seam for seven brothers...
...the eighth is at the same pit, too

Anyone who asks for Mr Lockwood at Woolley Colliery near Barnsley presents a problem. Eight Lockwoods work at the pit - all brothers.

Not only that, seven of them work in the same seam.

The Lockwood brothers have worked at Woolley for 25 years. It all started when two of them went to work as pit boys and found that they could earn a top class wage of 12s 6d a week.

They told the others, who soon followed. Said Mr Lawrence Lockwood, aged 57, of Burn Place, Athersley, Barnsley:

"I was one of the first to go to work at the pit. When I found I could earn such a good wage I told me brothers and they left their jobs to come to the pit. It was not long before all eight of us were working at Woolley and we have been there ever since."

The other seven brothers are: Vivian (57), Jonathan (49), Eric (42), all of Higham Common Road, Higham, near Barnsley, Byas (53) of Sykes Terrace, Higham, John (50) of Skelton Avenue, Staincross, Thomas (47)of Windhill Avenue, Staincross and William (42) of Greenside, Staincross.

Added Lawrence: "We are all so happy at the pit that I suppose we shall all work there until we retire."

Sheffield Telegraph, **Monday, September 4, 1961**

Lads rules

Uncle Bill and Uncle Frank were two of ar mam's brothers. Both Frank and Bill were a bit wayward. Maybe it was because they had another life as club and pub entertainers, or maybe they were just made that way.

Anyway, on this occasion the pit manager was having a meal in his office. The two uncles sneaked open the door and threw in a firework, then cleared off. When the banger went off the manager shot backwards off his chair but fell on the floor as the chair back stopped him.

He threw his knife and fork skywards. Both of them, apparently stuck in the ceiling and others in the room just stared.

Sounds implausible to me. But that's what I heard. I don't know why they targeted this poor bloke either. Maybe it's something as simple as the fact that he didn't eat in the canteen with all the other miners, I don't know.

Derek Tovey

Pit village life

There were two big huts at the bottom of the bus station, one contained big rolls of rubber belting for use in the pit, the other one was used as a bike shed for all the miners to keep their bikes safely whilst they were working.

One end of the bike shed was given to the Whittaker family to make into a shop to sell tobacco and cigarettes to the miners.

Miners would buy chewing tobacco, which they took down the pit to chew, probably to help with the dust, but there was an awful lot of spitting associated with chewing tobacco, and discoloured teeth. Eventually Mr Whittaker began all sorts of things and lots of people went to by from him.

I can remember No.3 shaft being built, that was the one nearest to the Old Low Row, when it was

finished I climbed to the top. But on reaching the top and looking down, got very scared. I had to shout and a man came up and took me down. I never went up again.

Flo Howard, nee Hayward

A welcome from Woolley

Flo Birkinshaw married a guy called John Winkler. Not much in that you may think. But John Winkler was a former German prisoner -of -war who was held at a prisoner-of-war camp at the far end of Woolley Edge during the Second World War. John was actually Rumanian, but had been living in Germany. He must have been a member of the German armed forces, but had no memories of how he had ended up in Woolley.

After the end of hostilities the prisoners were still kept in this country but of course were not as confined as they had been. John met Flo in the Woolley Welfare and when released, he married her and stayed on in Britain and later had two kids.

He lived with his family at Woolley Colliery until his death in 1959. I have very good memories of John Winkler. He was one hell of a nice man and I don't think I can remember anyone having anything bad to say about him. Sadly he was killed at Woolley Colliery after working a Saturday morning shift which he very rarely worked.

I got talking to Walt Birkinshaw who used to live at Woolley Colliery. He is now 76 and told me that some years ago and his wife were going on a touring holiday to Germany and took along with them a list of some of John Winkler's family who lived in Ausburg. He said that the expected few hours they hoped to spend with John's family turned into four days.

His story would have made a fantastic movie and a marvellous love story. John Winkler was one hell of a brave man to decide to stay in England, knowing just how much hostility there would be to a German living here. I have always had great admiration of him and I am sure so did a lot of other people.

Dave Bogg

Before Group 4... the Nightwatchman

Both my grandads worked at the pit. My dad's dad, Charles Rhodes, was night watchman.

His tools of the trade were a big stick and a bull terrier. The stick was no bother but the bull terrier was a bit of a handful.

A policeman visited about it biting someone and the dog behaved impeccably during the visit. The policeman commented on how well-behaved the dog was and how he could not understand the complaint etc. Unfortunately, when he got up to leave the dog bit him as well.

Don Rhodes

We'll never forget our four-legged friends

Pit ponies were a real presence in pit life. My grandfather, Charles Turner, had been head horse keeper for a group of pits, including Woolley Colliery.

He lived in the Top Row. His five sons worked in the stables as horse-keepers. My grandad used to buy pit ponies from all over the place, including trips to Germany and Poland in 1930. He also had the perk of a horse and trap for his private use... the 1930s equivalent of a company car, I suppose.

One of the horse-keeper's duties was obviously mucking out. One of my uncles used to smack the ponies on the behind with the shovel if they made a deposit on his shift.

This building started as the pit offices, and ended up as the canteen
(Margisons)

Outside the pit offices are office girls skipping in their break, including, Unknown, Barbara Landy, Unknown, Unknown, Kathy Douglas, and *front* Jen White
(Tears)

On the road, pit drivers waiting for instructions, with a front row of Eddie Booth, Herbert Sharp, Fred Crowther, Howard Hayes, Horace Cotton, Charlie Harrison and at the back, Len Naylor, Arthur Garforth and Doug Senior
(Boggs)

More winnings, but for what?
(United Villages)

WOOLLEY COLLIERY
WOOD SHIELD WINNERS
1935

Was the Wood Shield for first aid or rescue?
(United Villages)

Deputies' retirement dinner at Keresforth Hall in 1978, pictured are *left to right*, Mr and Mrs Viv Low, Mr and Mrs Friend Woodcock, Mr and Mrs John Bennett and Mr and Mrs Tommy Howarth
(Howarths)

Woolley Colliery - *Ar it woh*

Eventually, the ponies learned to hang on until the shift changed, when one of my other uncles would turn up to a full pile of steaming manure behind every pony.

Don Rhodes

Before I was old enough to go to school my mother let me go down to the stables, which were near the bottom of our garden, and sit with my uncles George and Albert, who looked after the pit ponies.

Sometimes a blacksmith called Charlie Ambler came to shoe the ponies and he used to have a joke with me. He stuck an old 3d piece to his forehead and said, "If you can guess what's under this 3d piece I'll give it to you." To which I replied, "A silly bugger." I can't remember if he gave me the 3d piece or not.

Stuart Rhodes

Barnsley Feast is coming and the pit ponies will be coming out of the pit and taken to the fields for two weeks, free from working down the mine.

We would wait outside the lamproom, across from the shaft. Out would come the first ponies from the cage. Daylight must have been a trigger for them, full of energy, kicking, snorting. Pony lads would lead them to the fields. Out of sight of the management we would jump on their backs and ride them. What a thrill! And I'm sure the ponies loved to stretch their legs and run free, instead of pulling tubs.

Ray Buckley

Cowboys at t'Colliery

Uncle Bill worked at the pit as a blacksmith. He later ran his own business making wrought iron work. In the 1940s, along with Uncle Frank, Uncle Ernest, Uncle Bill and Tommy Waller. They formed a musical group which raised to prominence as The Crossley Brothers. They appeared on the Kenneth Horne radio show, *Spot The Winner*, and also took part in *Carol Levis Discovery Show* at Barnsley Theatre.

Uncle Frank was employed at the pit top as a pony driver. Men led ponies which pulled tubs loaded with coal to the screens and the washer and back - these separated the coal from the slag in preparation for selling.

These drivers loved their ponies and boasted of their prowess at pulling loads faster and further than anybody else. They were competitive in the extreme. One day Uncle Frank challenged this other bloke to a race. He knew that he'd lose in a fair race but couldn't back down, so he did the next best thing. He got Uncle Bill to lend a hand.

Uncle Bill welded the wheels of the other bloke's tub to the rails. The two tubs were lined up ready next to each other. Uncle Frank made sure that his pony was harnessed to the un-welded tub and the contest began.

As Uncle Frank slowly trundled off with his tub-load of coal the other bloke, of course, couldn't make any head-way. His pony strained every sinew and started to work up a sweat. He slapped it, clapped it and bashed it but no amount of exhortation could make it move.

The pony gave one final mighty heave and the whole tub started to raise forwards into the air. Apparently Uncle Bill had welded the tub near to the end of two pieces of rail and the whole lot came up from the sleepers.

Encouraged by its success the pony carried on its forward momentum until the tub, plus its contents, raised up into the air, tilted forwards and emptied the coal onto the pony's back.

The pony panicked and the bloke spent the rest of the time trying to calm it down. The game was up. Everybody knew that Uncle Frank had cheated but it was so funny to the on-lookers that nobody minded at all. In fact it enhanced his standing quite a bit. Cheats never beat? You should have tried telling that to Uncle Frank.

Derek Tovey

In the blood, sweat and tears

My father Harry Metcalfe and his two brothers, Eddie and Horace, worked together all their life. They were born in Crigglestone Cottages, known as the 'milk and water row', in Holling Lane (Back Lane) in Crigglestone.

They started their working life at nearby Crigglestone pit, but not long after went to work at Woolley Colliery, and they finished their working life at Bullcliffe Colliery.

When they first started at Woolley Colliery they had to walk one and a half miles to Crigglestone station, get a train to Haigh, then walk about one half miles to the pit, do a shift of work, then do the same journey back again, fortified by a bottle of water and some fat and bread - no obesity problems in those days.

Eventually they clubbed together and bought an old Austin Seven, not many folk in Calder Grove had a car then, later they got a newer model.

It's funny what sticks in your mind - I can remember dad taking me into the canteen at Woolley Colliery where some of the men were drinking pints of milk. I said I would have one but dad said, "Have something smaller". I wanted what the men were having, so he got me one. Unfortunately it was going off, a bit sour and warm, but I wanted to be like the men so I drank it - ugh! I can taste it now.

I can remember dad taking me to look down the shaft at Woolley Colliery - it didn't attract me any - later he said, "we've enough miners in this family, we don't want anymore". So, although two of my cousins worked at Bullcliffe Colliery, I spent time in the RAF and Merchant Navy.

Recently my grandson was wanting to go to the Mining Museum, I said, "I'll pay but somebody else can take you down". I promised never to go down a pit and I'm not starting now, ("scaredy cat" he said).

My dad and his brothers died of pneumoconiosis, silicosis and chronic bronchitis. Perhaps the stone dust at Woolley Colliery contributed to this. I believe there was good money to be had there contracting, if you didn't mind the low seams and water.

Eddie died aged 55 years

Harry died aged 57 years

Horace died aged 53 years

My father and men like him and his brothers worked dammed hard to provide for their families and the country.

Colin Metcalfe

Strike pay

The miners were on strike in 1926, and nobody had any money. Some men qualified for relief, but had to pay it all back when they started back at work. Same with their rents, they all lived in pit

A rare underground photograph of Woolley pit deputies in the 1950s
(United Villages)

Riding the paddy train
(United Villages)

Pick the odd one out - no stick and a mucky face! Wonder why...
(United Villages)

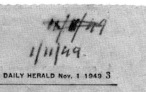

DAILY HERALD Nov. 1 1949 3

Joe (Old & Young) works on

Herald Reporter

BARNSLEY, Monday.

THEY are proud of Old Joe and Young Joe in the pits around here, for they are still going strong at Woolley Colliery after working, between them 117 years underground.

They have been pit mates ever since they found that they shared the name of Joe Senior, although unrelated.

Now they work within 100 yards of each other on the night shift, in charge of compressors.

OLD JOE, probably the country's oldest working miner, will be 81 in February. His wife died eight years ago and now he lives alone in Uplands-avenue, Kexbrough.

Trapped by fire

He has spent more than 50 years in the district's three collieries, in two of which he was trapped below ground by fires.

YOUNG JOE, only 78 at Christmas, has been even longer in the pits. He started as a boy of 11.

At his home in Pye-avenue, Mapplewell, he told me:

"When I was 11 and a half-timer, I started work at 6 a.m., worked until noon, and then went to school. Much of the year I never saw daylight until the week-end."

Joe Senior (left) and Joe 'Junior.'

Underground heroes
(Tears)

**My little pony - head horseman
Mr Turner with his devoted friend**
(United Villages)

On the pit top - no 1 and no 2 shaft - our playground
(Margisons)

Playground for some, work for others, new and old washer on the pit top
(Margisons)

houses so had to pay rent and a half until their arrears were cleared. Some men got casual farm work but not many. During the strike no-one had any coal, so the men dug out a 'dayhole' down the bottom of our gardens, and used to fetch coal out in bucketfuls. It was hard work but people were desperate for fuel to keep their families warm. On Saturdays while the strike was on, a few people got organised and made sandwiches and hot drinks for the children. We had to go to Woolley Colliery School for it. It was only plain but good with maybe a bun now and then.

Elizabeth Coatesworth, nee Wiles

Do they keep it in the bath?

I remember after dad died, mum began having problems getting coal up from the cellar and we couldn't always be there to carry the coal up for her, so she moved to a bungalow. When she moved her fuel allowance, which she had been promised for life, was stopped.

She was very upset. Dad had lost his life and this was her due. We tried to get her allowance back with no luck. We tried doctors and union reps and then one day my brother saw an M.P.'s surgery at Ossett Town Hall.

The M.P. was David Ginsberg, a Londoner put in a safe seat in Dewsbury. When my brother explained the 'fuel for life' being stopped and my mother not being able to cope with carrying coal from the cellar, Mrs Ginsberg, who was with her husband ,just couldn't believe it: "Do people still have coal in cellars? - old fires ? - face big bills? Darling,you really must speak to Derek (Ezra) about this."

Before the week was out, a letter from the Houses of Parliament to the area office got the matter sorted, thanks to Mrs Ginsberg's innocence.

Colin Metcalfe

Home comforts

I have fond memories of falling off walls and ingesting damp plaster on the semi-demolished Old Row a few years after we moved into the new house. Both top and bottom Old Rows had been built by the pit owners, Fountain and Burnley in the 19th century. Sadly they were built from local quarried sandstone from Woolley Edge.

You'd think that colliery engineers would realise that sandstone is porous wouldn't you? To compound this fault they seemed to think that a damp course was to make sure the building allowed water to track all the way to the roof space, and the ground floors were sandstone paving slabs. It was a bit like moving into a recently-emptied swimming pool. You had to be made of tough stuff to be a miner in those days, or a minor come to that.

Everything seemed to be in short supply. For years after the war goods were still rationed and only a pit employee whose name was on the rent book could receive concessionary coal.

Now Grandma thought this unfair because we had Uncle Bill living with us and he worked full time at the pit. One day Grandma marched westward to the pit offices just at the end of the row ready for a scrap.

Armed with her pinny and sleeves rolled up she went to the office of the then owner, Sir William Sutherland, one of whose minions explained procedures. Grandma, far from satisfied, started to storm out of the office when Sir William said something along the lines of, "So you see Mrs Crossley, it is not possible for you to receive any concessionary coal. You must pay the full rate of £16.00 per ton."

To this grandma replied, "I'll see thy bloody coffin dance afore I pay that."

This led to the local tradition of dads and mums taking babies for a nocturnal outing in their prams. They'd walk to the sidings (next to the stables, roughly where the local bus stop is now, or the other sidings just to the right of the lowest point of the road). Here babies were pulled out of their prams as they were filled with some of the best steam coal. Baby and blankets were then put back in the pram and the cargo quickly taken home. Soon after this dad gave up his job in Sheffield and started at the pit, so the coal was no longer an issue.

Living where we did you'd get used to the scrape and clop of boots and clogs as miners came to and left the pit along the bottom Old Row. Most of these travelled in 'Tracky' double deckers in the early mornings, early afternoons and late evenings as shifts changed.

Locals used the buses to get into Barnsley or Darton. The buses all carried a pall of blue smoke from the last desperate fags of the travelling miners and little puddles of spit and phlegm where they'd been inspecting the contents of their throats and lungs.

Grandma used the bus frequently and when mam was pregnant she'd be dragged along too so that she could be pushed to the front of the queues in Barnsley Market. On one occasion (without me mam) grandma was on the bus and it stopped to pick up Mrs B. at the Welfare.

Now Mrs B. was a bit of a snob, not the sort of thing you usually find on a pit bus. She was built like a stair-rod, carried her handbag in front of her like a sporran with a broken strap and wore a hat all the time, which, if red, made her look like a Swan Vesta. She also carried her C of E zeal about with her wherever she went and always had an opinion or an observation which she had to share.

On this occasion she asked grandma to move up in her seat to make room, despite the fact that other seats were free. She then followed this up with her observation along the lines of, "You know Mrs C., for people like you, who take up so much room, they ought to charge extra." Now this was about as silly as sneaking up from behind and scratching a boil on a pit pony's arse.

Grandma's riposte was quick and sharp:"If they charged by weight they wouldn't even stop to pick thee up." I'm not sure whether they carried on their journey in companionable silence or not.

Derek Tovey

This is the end

In 1958 the Old Row was finally pulled down. These houses must have stood there for at least 150 years as the stonework had become really badly-weathered. I was born on this street at No 6. In the mid-1940s some of my earliest memories are of pit clogs clomping on to the pit as the men came from off the pit buses. Although the pit head baths had been opened on the August 8, 1939 there were still a lot of men who did not use the baths.

The top Old Row was finally pulled down in 1971. With the closure of the two Old Rows Woolley Colliery had by then lost 60 families. This made life very difficult to support a shop and the fish and chip shop. These struggled on for a time, but with the closure of the pit in 1986 I guess this was the final curtain.

Dave Bogg

Miss Fountain cutting the sod for a new shaft
(Boggs)

West Side washery being blown up in 1993... going...going...going...going...gone
(Coatesworths)

Woolley Colliery - *Ar it woh*

Our contributors...

Dave Bogg
Granville Booth
Ray Buckley
Carol Brown, nee Shaw
Mick Brown
Joyce Parling, nee Brown
Olive Whittles, nee Brown
Patricia King, nee Coatesworth
Elizabeth Coatesworth, nee Wiles
Mavis Tomalic, nee Coatesworth
Marion Brackin, nee Coatesworth
Betty Lyman, nee Coatesworth
Phillip Crossley
Billy Crossley
George Crossley
Dennis Crossley
Kathleen Blackburn, nee Crossley
May Newton, nee Crossley
Neil Featherstone
Flo Howard
Tommy Howarth
Bob Hudson
Jenny Hepworth, nee Hudson
Jim Hudson
Jen James, nee White
Jean Jones, nee Rhodes
Ian King
Phil Margison
David Mason
Colin Metcalfe
Stuart Rhodes
Don Rhodes
Judy Speight, nee Tear
Doreen Sykes, nee Wraithmell
Mr and Mrs David Tovey
Derek Tovey
Flo White
Marjorie Whitehead, nee Child
Winnie Wood, nee Bowers

Conclusion

The Woolley Colliery of today is a village of two halves, on the one side the old Woolley Colliery with the two rows of pit houses and Bluebell Road, and on the other side a large estate of brand new houses.

The once Coal Board houses in the Low Row and Top Row are now mainly privately-owned and have been modernised to a high standard. Bluebell Road still has a few tenants of Barnsley Council, but several of these houses are now privately owned.

Woolley Colliery is a village with no amenities apart from a bus service to Barnsley. The school is a house, the church and institute have gone; there is no longer a shop in the village, residents have to travel to Darton and beyond for even the smallest item needed.

The paths up to the school and church, where countless generations trod are now overgrown and fenced off, even the sledging track has vanished. The school playing field where sports days and games were held is now part of the wood - with no sign of the happy times spent there.

The new housing estate with its houses of gleaming bricks and paintwork stands apart from the old village, never to have its pristine exteriors sullied and sooted from the dirt belching out of the long-gone mine, nor its peace disturbed by the shift buzzer. Maybe not even the name will be same.

Hopefully, when all building work is complete and the new roads opened to everyone, it will be the children from both communities who, by playing together, will be the catalyst which will unite the village. They are not judgemental and have no prejudices. Like us, they'll play.

Joyce Parling, nee Brown